iPhone 8 Gui

The iPhone Manual for Beginners, Seniors & for All iPhone Users

(The Simplified Manual for Kids and Adults)

Dale Brave

ISBN: 978-1-63750-240-2

Table of Contents

Introduction

The iPhone 8 and iPhone 8 Plus are faster than ever and have more powerful cameras. With the latest edition of this bestselling guide, you get a funny, simplified guide to the tips, shortcuts, and workarounds that will turn you into an iPhone master.

For those who want the most sophisticated technology available in a mobile phone, but without a sky-high price, the iPhone 8 and iPhone 8 Plus is perfect for you.

Millions of people all over the world are excited about this iPhone 8 and iPhone 8 Plus, simply because the iPhone offers many advance and exciting features, including a *camera like no other*, *Siri*, turn-by-turn driving directions, a calendar, and a lot more. But if you're acquiring the iPhone 8 and iPhone 8 Plus, for the first time, or you probably need more information on how to use your device optimally, that is why this book is your best choice of guide.

In this book you'll discover:

• How to set up your brand new iPhone

- iPhone 8 Series Security Features

- Apple Face ID Hidden Features

- All iPhone 8 Gestures you should know

- How to Hide SMS notification content display on iPhone screen

- Software & hardware features of iPhone 8

- Top iPhone gestures and shortcuts

- Detailed camera app tutorials

- The secrets of mastering mobile photography

- Troubleshooting tips

- How to use the virtual Home button

- How to enable limited USB settings

- Best Shortcuts you are never aware of

- Disabling Location-Based iAds

- How to Use Look Around feature in Apple Maps

- How to Customize Your Memoji and Animoji

- How to Use the New Gestures for Copy, Cut, Paste, Redo and Undo

- How to Use Cycle Tracking in Health

...and a lot more.

It is the perfect guide for all iPhone users, as you would get simplified follow-through in-depth tips and tutorials on every possible thing you should know about iPhone 8 and iPhone 8 Plus.

Chapter 1

iPhone 8 and iPhone 8 Plus: What You Ought to Know

Announced at precisely the same time as the iPhone X, the iPhone 8 and iPhone 8 Plus might appear just a little overshadowed by their fancy new sibling. Sure they don't have all the elegant top features of the iPhone X, but to state that the iPhone 8 and iPhone 8 Plus aren't perfect iPhones and can't keep their own, is incorrect.

The coolest new top features of the iPhone 8 and iPhone 8 Plus Coming just one single year following the iPhone 7 and iPhone 7 Plus, it might be easy to presume the update to the iPhone 8 and iPhone 8 Plus would be small, even if it's a welcomed one. From a distance, you might also mistake the iPhone 8 for the iPhone 7, but under the display, there are significant improvements.

- **iPhone 8 Processors**

The first among these improvements is the cutting-edge, 64-bit, multicore A11 Bionic processor chip, and an all-new Images Processing Device. These chips deliver major HP for processing- and graphics-intensive jobs. The iPhone 7 series was built around powerful chips; however, the A11 Bionic is 25% percent to 70% faster than the iPhone 7's A10 Fusion chip, relating to Apple. *How fast?* In some instances, the A11 is faster than its predecessors.

The iPhone 8's GPU is approximately 30% faster than

the main one in the iPhone 7 series; that GPU is utilized for the camera and Apple's execution of augmented fact. The camera on the iPhone 8 seems superficially exactly like that on the iPhone 7. It requires 12-megapixel images and catches 4K video, but those specifications don't meet up the iPhone 8's improvements.

- **iPhone 8 Cameras**

The iPhone 8's camera system allows 83% more light into its sensor, leading to better low-light pictures and more true-to-life colors. Around the iPhone 8 Plus, this allows a new Family portrait mode, where the camera senses light and depth as you compose a picture and dynamically adjusts to produce the best-looking image.

Video saving is nicely boosted too. The 8 series can catch 4K video at up to 60 fps (up from 30 fps on the 7) and slow-motion, 240-frame-per-second video in 1080p (in comparison to 120 fps on the 7).

- **<u>Augmented Reality</u>**

The iPhone 8's GPU is also necessary to its Augmented Reality features. Augmented Fact or AR, combines live data from the web with images of the real-world in front of you (like viewing Pokemon apparently in your living room in Pokemon Go). AR takes a private camera to ensure it works wherever you are and in whatever conditions, and a powerful GPU for merging data, live images, and digital animations. The excess HP under the iPhone 8's hood and cleverness included in its digital cameras make the iPhone 8 suitable to AR.

- **iPhone 8 Design and Wireless Charging**

As the iPhone 8 and iPhone 8 Plus appear to be recent versions of the iPhone, they will vary. Eliminated is the aluminium back, changed with an all-new cup back. And, despite what sceptics might state, it isn't to help Apple get additional money from broken cup sections. It's for providing power.

Thanks to the glass back, the iPhone 8 and iPhone 8 Plus enable inductive charging (also known as *wi-fi charging*

despite, you understand, needing a cable). With it, you can neglect plugging in your iPhone to charge it. Just place the iPhone on a radio charging mat, and power moves from a wall structure store through the charging mat into the phone's electric battery. Predicated on the trusted Qi standard, it will eventually be easy to charge the iPhone 8 at home or on the go in international airports and other locations.

In case your charging mat is linked to power through USB-C, the fast-charging feature provides iPhone 8 a 50% charge in only 30 minutes. iPhone 8 and iPhone 8 Plus Glass back permits inductive charging. It is considerably faster and with more power-efficient CPU. Also, with an improved GPU Camera for truer-to-live colour catch and allows more light.

The video camera catches 4K at 60 fps.

What Occurred to the iPhone 7S?

Never someone to shy from breaking custom, Apple's skipped the old naming convention that's existed for almost six years. Before, Apple gets the apple iPhone 4 then your iPhone 4S. The iPhone 5, then iPhone 5S. Completely until 2016.

So, following that reasoning, the iPhone 8 should be called the iPhone 7S. Instead, Apple decided to miss an 'S' and go to the next model. In any event, don't go searching for an iPhone 7S; you may never find it.

iPhone 8 - Top Features

After months of rumours, leaking, and lots of speculation, the iPhone 8 has finally been unveiled. This latest flagship smartphone as at 2017 was proven to the world throughout a major keynote at Apple's new HQ in Cupertino the other day. The iPhone 8 and much larger iPhone 8 Plus both add several improvements over their predecessors, making them the best Apple smartphones as when newly released.

Alongside the iPhone 8, the united states technology also primarily revealed its iPhone X that includes a new design with a display that covers the whole front of these devices. However, with a £999 price, and a release time of November 2018, the iPhone X would be out.

1. **Wireless Charging**

Apple has included wifi charging on its latest smartphone; this means it can get a fill-up by merely being placed on the compatible pad. The iPhone 8 uses the established Qi ecosystem; this means it will use most accessories available on the marketplace.

It's well worth noting that Apple doesn't add a charging pad in the package, so you should buy one separately to utilize this new feature. As well as wireless charging, the iPhone 8 can have its battery boosted in super-quick time. A fresh Apple-designed image signal processor provides advanced pixel processing, wide colour capture, faster autofocus in low light and better HDR photos, while a fresh quad-LED True Tone Flash with Decrease Sync leads to more uniformly lit backgrounds and foregrounds.

Apple says that this results in outstanding photos with vibrant, realistic colours and greater detail. The iPhone 8

Plus retains its dual-lens camera, which, along using its smart zoom and Family portrait Mode, is now able to change the light in pictures.

Portrait Light brings dramatic studio room lights to the iPhone, allowing customers to fully capture stunning portraits with a shallow depth-of-field impact in five different light styles.

2. *A11 Bionic Processor*

Apple's boosting its new processor chip is the quickest ever to be observed within an iPhone. The brand new *A11 Bionic chip* has around 30% faster graphics performance than the prior brains found inside the iPhone 7. If true it's more likely to outperform not only its predecessor but all the latest Google android competition in the year 2017 and early 2018.

3. *New Colors & Cup Design*

Apple has included some new colours on the iPhone 8 with these devices happening sale in space grey, gold, and silver. The iPhone 8 and iPhone 8 Plus also introduce a lovely cup back design and do not worry about any of it breaking as Apple says it is the most durable cup ever in a smartphone.

It is manufactured utilizing a seven-layer colour process for precise hue and opacity, delivering a rich depth of colour with a colour-matched aerospace-grade aluminium bezel. Both iPhone 8 and iPhone 8 Plus are also water and dust resistant.

4. *Extra Storage*

There's some good news if you are always working out of space for storage as Apple has included 64GB as standard. That is double the essential memory on the iPhone 7. Apple, in addition, has ditched the 128GB version with the iPhone 8 featuring 256GB of in-built memory space.

It's also worthy of noting that iOS 11, which launches in a few days, will automatically decrease the size of photos taken on the iPhone's camera, providing users even more extra space.

5 Interesting iPhone 8 Features

1. *AR - Augmented Reality*

This virtually is the most impressive new feature of the iPhone 8 because of its ability to use augmented reality (AR) apps. They don't need multiple digital cameras or sensors to operate. AR applications rely on the iPhone 8's back camera.

Since AR technology continues to be relatively new rather than so trusted, the amount of applications using AR is continually increasing. AR offers a new way for individuals to play video games, learn, and shop. It's also useful in everyday living: you may use AR to, for example, measure things quickly without a tape measure.

The world-famous furniture merchant IKEA, also, has launched its AR app. IKEA Place provides 3D types of IKEA furniture and allows an individual to put them in real-world environments; This implies you don't have to buy a couch or seat and transport to your living room to see whether it suits or not. You can merely use the IKEA application to learn. The app also allows users to buy and order products.

2. *Powerful Picture Editing*

The iPhone 8 features Apple's powerful new A11 Bionic processor and a better camera. These characteristics make the iPhone 8 a great tool even for professional photographers. The App Store has a vast assortment of picture editing apps. Using the right apps, you may make your photos look superb and professional. Among my favorites is **Photofox**. It combines the simplicity of mobile editing and enhancing with the energy and countless top features of desktop apps, such as *Adobe Photoshop.*

The app helps you to edit images in levels, which can be an important function in professional picture editing. Creating unique designs with visual elements is uncomplicated and straightforward. The application is free but contains in-app purchases.

3. *4K Video*

The iPhone 8's camera has become powerful smartphone

cameras in the marketplace. Among its most exceptional features is its capability to take 4K video at 60 fps. What's more, the iPhone 8 can also record excellent gradual movement video at 240 fps with 1080p resolution. If you wish to customize your iPhone's camera configurations, go to *Settings > Camera.*

4. *Portraits with Portrait Lighting*

Apple introduced the astonishing Family portrait photo setting in the iPhone 7 Plus. The iPhone 8 Plus will take things to another level with Family portrait Lighting.

In brief, Family portrait photo mode gives you razor-sharp portrait photos of your subject matter with a blurry background. The iPhone 8 Plus, however, provides you with the choice of adding special lights like in real a studio room. The very best part is that once you've taken a picture using Portrait mode, you can still change the lighting settings afterwards to make your picture look the same as you want to buy too.

You can customize the light settings of the portrait picture you already took simply by tapping *Edit* on the picture in the Photos app. The Family portrait Lighting wheel should come up, which you can slide to change the image configurations.

5. Screen Recording

The brand new iPhones include native screen recording built-in - there's no dependence on third-party apps; this new feature comes in the iPhone's Control Centre, which you can access by swiping up from underneath the screen. The display documenting icon is not in the Control Centre by default; you will need to add it by heading to the iPhone's configurations/settings page.

C h a p t e r   2

How to Set up Your brand-new iPhone 8

For many individuals, the iPhone 8 Series would radically not be the same as the previous iPhone model. Not surprisingly, the iPhone set up process hasn't transformed much. However, you might end up on the familiar ground; you may still find a lot of little things you honestly must do before you switch ON your new phone for the very first time (or soon after that).

Let's check out how to set up your brand-new iPhone 8 the proper way.

Setup iPhone 8 the Correct Way

With iPhone 8, you'll have the ability to take benefit of Apple's Automatic Setup. If you're on an updated iPhone without Face Identification, you would see that Touch ID is entirely gone. (Which means you'll save one face, rather than several.)

If you're a serial upgrader, and you're from the year-old

iPhone 6, less has changed. But you'll still need to update just as usual.

iPhone 8 Set up: The Fundamentals

Re-download only the applications you would need; that one is crucial. Most of us have so many applications on our iPhones that people do not use; this is the big reason we execute a clean set up, in all honesty. Utilize the App Store application and make sure you're authorized into the Apple accounts. (Touch the tiny icon of the Updates - panel to see which accounts you're logged on to.) Only download applications you've found in the past half a year. Or, be daring: download stuff you Utilize regularly. We're prepared to wager it'll be considered a very few.

Set up **DO NOT Disturb** - If you're like ordinary people, you're constantly getting notifications, iMessages, and other types of distractions through to your iPhone. Create **DO NOT Disturb** in the Configurations application (it's in the next section listed below, slightly below *Notifications* and *Control Centre*). You'll want to routine it for occasions when you need never to be bothered.

Toggle Alarm to On and then Messages when you want to keep Notifications away from that person. Try 9 p.m. to 8 a.m. when you can.

Pro suggestion: *Let some things through if there's an Emergency: Enable Allow Phone calls From your Favorites and toggle Repeated Phone calls to On. iOS 13 also enables you to switch on DO NOT Disturb at Bedtime, which mutes all notifications and even hides them from the lock screen, and that means you don't get distracted when you take the phone to check the time.*

Auto Setup for iPhone 8

Secondly; Auto Setup enables you to duplicate your Apple ID and home Wi-Fi configurations from another device, simply by getting them close collectively.

In case your old iPhone (or iPad) has already been operating iOS 12 or iOS 13, to put it simply the devices next to one another. Then follow the prompts to avoid needing to enter your Apple ID and Wi-Fi passwords;

this makes the original iPhone set up much smoother.

Set up a fresh iPhone 8 from Scratch

The guide below assumes you're establishing your brand-new iPhone from scratch. If you don't wish to accomplish that, you'll need to read further.

Restoring from a back-up of Your old iPhone

You'll probably be restoring your brand-new iPhone from a back-up of your present iPhone. If that's so, then you merely want to do a couple of things:

- Be sure you come with an up-to-date backup.

- Use Apple's new Auto Setup feature to get you started.

The first thing is as simple as going to the iCloud configurations on your iPhone, and looking at that, they're surely a recent automated back-up. If not, do one by hand. Head to *Configurations > Your Name > iCloud > iCloud Back-up and tap **BACKUP Now**.* Wait around until it is done.

Set up Face ID

Face ID is much simpler to use than Touch ID, and it's

also simpler to create.

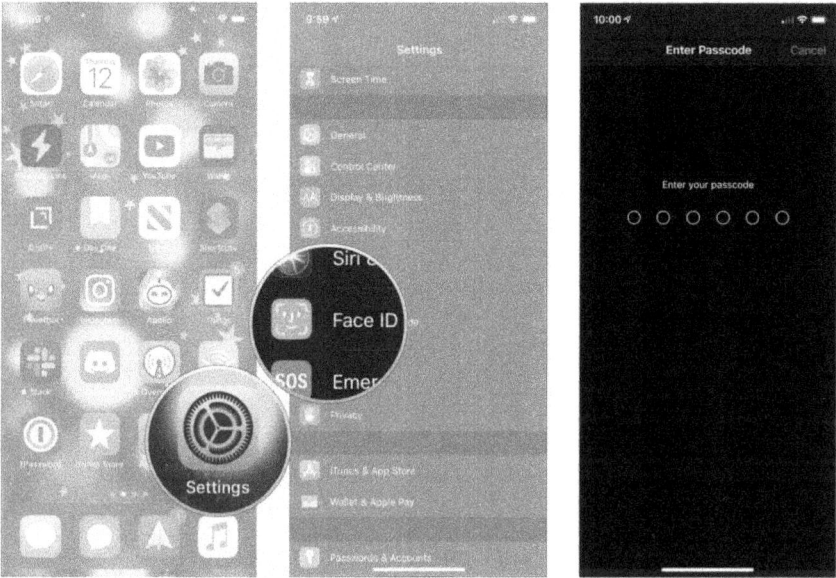

Instead of needing to touch your iPhone with your fingerprints, one at a time, you simply check out the camera, and that's almost it. To create Face ID on your iPhone, do the next when prompted through the preliminary iPhone setup. (If you'd like to begin over with a phone you set up previously, check out *Settings > Face ID & Passcode, and type in your password, to begin.*)

Establishing Face ID is similar to the compass calibration your iPhone enables you to do from time to time when you use the Maps app. Only rather than rolling the iPhone around, you turn your head. You'll need to do two scans, and then the iPhone 8 would have your 3D head stored in its Secure Enclave, inaccessible to anything, even to iOS itself (despite some clickbait "news" stories).

Now, still, in Settings/*Configurations* > *Face ID & Passcode*, you can pick which features to use with Face ID, as everyone else did with *Touch ID*.

If you regularly sport another appearance - you're a clown, a doctor, an impersonator, or something similar - then additionally, you should create another impression. Just tap the button in the facial ID settings to set this up.

Create iPhone Email

- *Add your email accounts* - Whether you utilize Mail, Perspective, or something similar to Sparrow, you'll want to include your email accounts immediately. For Apple's Email app, touch *Configurations* > *Accounts & Passwords, then tap*

Add Accounts. Choose your email supplier and follow the steps to enter all the knowledge required.

- **See more email preview** - Email lets you start to see the content of a note without starting it. May as well see as a lot of it as you possibly can, right? Utilize Settings > Email and tap on the Preview button. Change your configurations to five lines and get more information from your email messages and never have to get them open up.

- **Established your default accounts** - For reasons unknown, our iOS Email settings always appear to default to a merchant account we never use, like **iCloud**. Tap *Configurations >   Accounts & Passwords > Your email accounts name, and then touch Accounts >   Email*. Once you reach the depths of the settings, you can touch your preferred email; this would be your address in new mails. (When there is only one address in here, you're all set.) That is also the spot to add some other email addresses associated with your email account.

Advanced iPhone Email tweaks

- *Swipe to control email* - It's much more helpful to have the ability to swipe your email messages away rather than clicking through and tapping on several control keys. Swipe to Archive, so that whenever you swipe that path, you'll have the ability to either quickly save a contact to your Archive. Or, if your email accounts support swiping left as a default Delete action, it'll offer a Garbage icon. Swipe left to Tag as Read, which is a smart way to slam through your electronic mails as you have them. This only impacts your built-in Email application from Apple. Each third-party email customer can do things differently.

- *Add an HTML signature* - A sound email signature really can cause you to look professional, so make sure to include an HTML signature to your email. If you've already got one on the desktop, duplicate and paste the code into contact and ahead to yourself.

You'll be able to copy and paste it into an Email application (or whichever email supplier you like, if it facilitates it). It could be as easy as textual content formatting tags or as complicated as adding a logo design from a webserver. You should use an iOS application to make one, too; however, they tend to look fairly basic.

Manage Calendars, iCloud, Communications and more

- *Set default Calendar alert times* - Calendar is ideal for alerting you to important occasions, but it's not necessarily at a convenient or useful time. Established the default timing on three types of occasions: Birthdays, Occasions, and All-Day Occasions, and that means you get reminders when they're helpful. Utilize *Configurations > Calendars*. Tap on Default Alert Times and set your Birthday reminders to 1 day before, your Occasions to quarter-hour before (or a period which makes more sense to your mind), and All-

Day Occasions on the day of the function (10 a.m.). You'll never miss a meeting again.

- *Background application refresh* - You'll desire to be selective about which applications you desire to be in a position to run in the background, so have a look at the list in *Settings > General > Background App Refresh*. Toggle Background App Refresh to ON, then toggle OFF all the applications you don't need being able to access anything in the background. When in question, toggle it to OFF and find out if you are slowed up by any applications that require to refresh when you release them. You'll want to allow Background Refresh for Cult of Macintosh Magazine!

Secure Your Web Experience

- *Browser set up* - Surfing the net is filled with forms to complete. Adding your name, address, email, and bank cards may take up a great deal of your power. Make sure to head into

Configurations > Browser > AutoFill to create your mobile internet browser the proper way. First, toggle Use Contact Info to On. Then tap on My Info and select the contact you want to use when you encounter form areas in Browser. Toggle Titles and Passwords on as well, and that means you can save that across appointments to the same website. (This pulls from *iCloud Keychain*, so make sure to have that allowed, too.)

Toggle *CREDIT CARDS* to ON as well, which means you can shop swiftly. (*be sure only to use SSL-encrypted websites.*)

Pro suggestion: Manage which bank cards your iPhone helps you to save with a tap on BANK CARDS. You can include new cards within, or delete ones that no more work or that you don't want to use via mobile Browser.

The browser in iOS 13 and later version also blocks cross-site monitoring, which are those cookies that follow you around and let online stores place the same advertisements on every subsequent web page you visit.

That is On by default, and that means you should not do anything. Just relax and revel in your newfound personal privacy.

iCloud Everywhere

- *iCloud is everything* - There's without a doubt in our thoughts that iCloud is the easiest, optimum solution for keeping all of your stuff supported and safe. Utilize the Configurations > iCloud and be sure to register with your **Apple ID**. You can manage your storage space in here, but make sure to enable all you need immediately. Enable iCloud Drive, Photos, Connections, Reminders, Browser, Records, News, Wallet, Back-up, Keychain and others once you get the iPhone unpacked. You can enable Email and Calendars if you merely use Apple's applications and services; usually, you would keep those toggled OFF.

Services subscription during iPhone setup

- *Enable iCloud Photo Library* - We love the iCloud Photo Library. It maintains your photos and videos securely stored in the cloud and enable you to get full-quality copies of your documents in the event you misplace your originals. iCloud Picture Library depends on your iCloud storage space, if you have a lot of photos, you'll want to bump that up. Utilize Configurations > iCloud > Photos, then toggle iCloud Image Library to On. (Remember that this will switch off My Picture Stream. If you'd like both, you'll need to re-toggle Image Stream back again to On.)

- *Use iTunes Match* - Sure, Apple Music monitors all the music data files on your devices, but if you delete them from your iPhone and don't have a back-up elsewhere, you're heading to have to stay for whatever quality Apple Music will provide you with when you listen. If you wish to maintain your full-resolution music documents supported to the cloud, use iTunes Match.

You get all of your music files matched up or published to iCloud in the best bitrate possible. After that, you can stream or download the music to any device provided your iTunes Match membership is intact. Never be without your music (or have an over-filled iPhone) again. Go to *Configurations > Music*. Then touch on Sign up to iTunes Match to understand this valuable service allowed on your brand-new iPhone.

More iPhone set up Tweaks

- *Extend your Auto-Lock* - Let's face it. The default two minutes you get for the Volume of time your iPhone would remain on without turning off its screen may keep the battery higher much longer, but it's insufficient for anybody during regular use. Utilize Configurations, General, Auto-Lock to create this to the whole five minutes, which means you can stop tapping your screen at all times to keep it awake.

- *Get texts everywhere* - You can enable your Mac PC or iPad to get texts from your iPhone, provided you've set up iMessage to them (Settings, Text messages, toggle iMessage to ON on any iOS device, Messages Preferences on your Mac). Ensure that your other device is close by when you Utilize Settings on your iPhone, then touch Messages > TEXT Forwarding. Any devices available will arrive on the list. Toggle your Mac or iPad to On, and then check the prospective device for a code. Enter that code into your iPhone. Now all of your devices are certain to get not only iMessages but also texts from those not using iMessage.

- *Equalise your tunes* - Start the EQ in your Music application to be able to hear your preferred jams and never have trouble with a Bluetooth speaker. Go to Configurations > Music. Once there, touch on EQ and established your iPhone to NIGHT TIME; this will provide you with a great quantity rise for those times where you want to blast *The Clash* while you make a quick supper in the kitchen.

Restoring iPhone 8 Backup from iCloud and iTunes

There is no need connecting your brand-new iPhone to your personal computer, as long as there is a mobile data connection designed for activation.

As you end the set-up wizard, you may navigate back by tapping the back arrow at the top left-hand side of the screen and scroll further to another display by tapping another button at the top right-hand corner.

You can commence by pressing down the power button at the top edge of your brand-new iPhone. You may want to keep it pressed down for about two seconds until you notice a vibration, meaning the iPhone is booting up.

Once it boots up finally, you can start initial set up by following the processes below;

- Swipe your finger over the display screen to start the set-up wizard.

- Choose the language of preference - English is usually at the top of the list, so there is no problem finding it. However, if you would like to apply a different language, scroll down to look for your desired *language,* and tap to select the preferred language.

- Choose your **Country** - the *United States,* for instance, which may be close to the top of the list. If otherwise, scroll down the list and select the United States or any of your choice.

- You need to connect your iPhone to the internet to start its activation. You can test this via a link with a Wi-Fi network. Locate the name of your available network in the list shown, and then tap on it to select it.

- Enter the Wi-Fi security password (you will generally find this written on your router, which is probably known as the WPA Key, WEP Key, or

Password) and select Sign up. A tick indication shows you are connected, and a radio image appears near the top of the screen. The iPhone would now start activation with Apple automatically. It may take some time!

- In case your iPhone is a 4G version, you would be requested to check for updated internet configurations after inserting a new Sim card. You can test this anytime, so, for the present time, tap **Continue**.

- Location services would help you with mapping, weather applications, and more, giving you specific information centred wholly on what your location is. Select whether to use location service by tapping to *allow location services.*

- You would now be requested to create **Touch ID,** which is Apple's fingerprint identification. **Touch ID** allows you to unlock your iPhone with your fingerprint instead of your passcode or security password. To set up Tap Identification, put a finger or your thumb on the home button (but do not press it down!). To by-pass this for the moment, tap *setup Touch ID later*.

- If you are establishing Touch ID, the tutorial instruction on the screen will walk you through the set-up process. Put your finger on the home button, then remove it till the iPhone has properly scanned your fingerprint. Whenever your print is wholly scanned, you would notice a screen letting you know that tap recognition is successful. Tap **Continue**.

- You would be requested to enter a passcode to secure your iPhone. If you create **Touch ID**, you must use a passcode if, in any case, your fingerprint isn't acknowledged. Securing your computer data is an excellent idea, and the iPhone provides you with several options. Tap password option to choose your lock method.

- You can arrange a Custom Alphanumeric Code (that is a security password that uses characters and figures), a Custom Numeric Code (digit mainly useful, however, you can add as many numbers as you want!) or a 4-Digit Numeric Code. In case you didn't install or set up **Touch ID,** you may even have an option not to add a Security password. Tap on your selected Security option.

- I would recommend establishing a 4-digit numeric code, or Touch ID for security reasons, but all optional setup is done likewise. Input your selected Security password using the keyboard.

- Verify your Security password by inputting it again. If the Password does not match, you'll be requested to repeat! If indeed they do match, you'll continue to another display automatically.

At this time of the set-up process, you'll be asked whether you have used an iPhone before and probably upgrading it, you can restore all of your applications and information from an iCloud or iTunes backup by deciding on the best option. If this is your first iPhone, you would have to get it started as new, yet, in case you are moving from Android to an iPhone, you can transfer all your data by deciding and choosing the choice you want.

How to Move Data From an Android Phone

Apple has made it quite easy to move your data from a Google Android device to your new iPhone.

Proceed to the iOS app. I'll direct you about how to use the application to move your data!

- Using the iPhone, if you are on the applications & data screen of the set-up wizard, tap *move data from Google android*.

- Go to the Play Store on your Google android

device and download the app recommended by the set-up wizard. When it is installed, open up the app, select **Continue,** and you'll be shown the *Terms & Conditions* to continue.

- On your Android device, tap *Next* to start linking your Devices. On your own iPhone, select *Continue*.

- Your iPhone would show a 6-digit code that has to be received into the **Google android** device to set the two phones up.

- Your Google android device would screen all the data that'll be moved. By default, all options are ticked - so if there could be something you don't want to move, tap the related collection to deselect it. If you are prepared to continue, tap *Next* on your Google android device.

- As the change progresses, you would notice the iPhone display screen changes, showing you the position of the info transfer and progress report.

- When the transfer is completed, you will notice a confirmation screen on each device. On your Android Device, select *Done* to shut the app. On your own iPhone, tap **Continue**.

- An **Apple ID** allows you to download apps, supported by your iPhone and synchronize data through multiple devices, which makes it an essential account you should have on your iPhone! If you have been using an iPhone previously, or use iTunes to download music to your laptop, then you should have already become an *Apple ID* user. Register with your username and passwords (when you have lost or forgotten your Apple ID or password, you will see a link that may help you reset it). If you're not used to iPhone, select doesn't have an Apple ID to create one for free.

- The Terms & Conditions for your iPhone can be seen. Please go through them (tapping on more to study additional info), so when you are done, tap **Agree**.

- You'll be asked about synchronizing your data with iCloud. That's to ensure bookmarks, connections, and other items of data are supported securely with your other iPhone data. Tap **merge** to permit this or **don't merge** if you'll have a choice to keep your details elsewhere asides iCloud.

- **Apple pay** is Apple's secure payment system that stores encrypted credit or debit card data on your device and making use of your iPhone also with your fingerprint to make safe transactions online and with other apps. Select *Next* to continue.

- To *feature/add a card*, place it on a set surface and place the iPhone over it, so the card is put in the camera framework. The credit card info would be scanned automatically, and you would be requested to verify that the details on display correspond with your card. You'll also be asked to enter the *CVV* (safety code) from the personal strip behind the card. If you choose (or the camera cannot recognize your cards), you can enter credit card information by hand by tapping the hyperlink. You could bypass establishing **Apple Pay** by tapping *create later*.

- Another screen discusses the *iCloud keychain*, which is Apple's secure approach to sharing your preserved security password and payment information throughout all your Apple devices. You might use *iCloud security code* to validate your brand-new device and import present data, or you might be asked to continue registering your keychain if it's your first Apple device. In case you don't want to share vital data with other devices, you should go to *avoid iCloud keychain* or *don't restore passwords*.

- If you want to set up your Apple keychain, you'd be notified to either uses a Security password (the same one you'd set up on your iPhone or produce a different code. If you're making use of your iCloud security code, you should put it on your iPhone when prompted.

- This would confirm your ID when signing on to an iCloud safety code; a confirmation code would be delivered via SMS. You may want to hyperlink your smartphone text code (if you have never distributed one with Apple already) so that the code may be provided as a text. Then enter this code to your iPhone if requested, then select *Next.*

- You'll then be asked to create **Siri**. *Siri* is your

own digital personal associate, which might search the internet, send communications, and check out data in your device and a lot more, all without having to flick via specific apps. Choose to create Siri by tapping the choice or start Siri later to skip this task for now.

- To set up and create SIRI, you would need to speak several phrases to the iPhone to review your conversation patterns and identify your voice.

- Once you say every term, a tick would be observed, showing that it's been known and comprehended. Another phrase may indicate that you should read aloud.

- Once you've completed the five phrases, you would notice a display notifying that Siri has been set up correctly. Tap *Continue*.

- The iPhone display alters the colour balance to help make the screen show up naturally under distinctive light conditions. You can switch this off in the screen settings after the iPhone has completed configuring it. Tap *continue* to continue with the setup.

- Has your iPhone been restored? Tap begin to transfer your computer data to your brand-new iPhone.

- You'll be prompted to ensure your brand-new iPhone has enough power to avoid the device turning off in the process of downloading applications and information. Tap *OK* to verify this recommendation.

- You would notice a notification show up on your apps to download in the background.

NB: Setting up any new iPhone model: A similar method, as described above, applies.

How to Restore iPhone 8 Back-up from iCloud or iTunes

If you want to restore your iPhone from an iTunes back-up, you may want to connect to iCloud and have the latest version of iTunes installed on it. If you are ready to begin this process, tap **restore** from iTunes back-up on your iPhone and connect it to your personal computer. Instructions about how to bring back your data can be followed on the laptop screen.

In case your old iPhone model was supported on iCloud, then follow the instructions below to restore your applications & data to your brand-new device:

- Tap *Restore* from iCloud back-up.
- Register with the Apple ID and Password that you applied to your old iPhone. If you fail to recollect the security password, there's a link that may help

you reset it.

- The Terms & Conditions screen would show. Tap the links to learn about specific areas in detail. When you are ready to proceed, select **Agree**.

- Your iPhone would need some moments to create your Apple ID and hook up with the iCloud server.

- You would notice a summary of available backups to download. The most up-to-date backup would be observed at the very top, with almost every other option below it. If you want to restore from a desirable backup, tap the screen for *all backups* to see the available choices.

- Tap on the back-up you want to restore to start installing.

- A progress bar would be shown, providing you with a demo of the advancement of the download. When the restore is completed, the device will restart.

- You would see a notification telling you that your iPhone is updated effectively. Tap *Continue*.

- To complete the iCloud set up on your recently restored iPhone, you should re-enter your iCloud

(Apple ID) password. Enter/review it and then tap *Next*.

- You'll be prompted to upgrade the security information related to your ***Apple ID***. Tap on any stage to replace your computer data, or even to bypass this option. If you aren't ready to do this, then tap the ***Next*** button.

- **Apple pay** is Apple's secure payment system that stores encrypted credit or debit card data on your device and making use of your iPhone also with your fingerprint to make safe transactions online and with other apps. Select ***Next*** to continue.

- To ***feature/add a card***, place it on a set surface and place the iPhone over it, so the card is put in the camera framework. The credit card info would be scanned automatically, and you would be requested to verify that the details on display correspond with your card. You'll also be asked to enter the ***CVV*** (safety code) from the personal strip behind the card. If you choose (or the camera cannot recognize your cards), you can enter credit card information by hand by tapping the hyperlink.

You could bypass establishing **Apple Pay** by tapping *create later*.

- Another screen discusses the *iCloud keychain*, which is Apple's secure approach to sharing your preserved security password and payment information throughout all your Apple devices. You might use *iCloud security code* to validate your brand-new device and import present data, or you might be asked to continue registering your keychain if it's your first Apple device. In case you don't want to share vital data with other devices, you should go to *avoid iCloud keychain* or *don't restore passwords*.

- If you selected to set up your Apple keychain, you'd be notified to either uses a Security password (the same one you'd set up on your iPhone) or provide a different code. If you're making use of your iCloud security code, you should put it on your iPhone when prompted.

- This would confirm your ID when signing on to an iCloud safety code; a confirmation code would be delivered via SMS. You may want to hyperlink your smartphone text code (if you have never distributed one with Apple already) so that the code may be provided as a text. Then enter this code to your iPhone if requested, then select *Next.*

- You'll then be asked to create **Siri**. *Siri* is your own digital personal associate, which might search the internet, send communications, and check out data in your device and a lot more, all without having to flick via specific apps. Choose to create Siri by tapping the choice or start Siri later to skip this task for now.

- To set up and create SIRI, you would need to speak several phrases to the iPhone to review your conversation patterns and identify your voice.

- Once you say every term, a tick would be observed, showing that it's been known and comprehended. Another phrase may indicate that you should read aloud.

- Once you've completed the five phrases, you would notice a display notifying that Siri has been set up correctly. Tap *Continue*.

- The iPhone display alters the colour balance to

help make the screen show up naturally under distinctive light conditions. You can switch this off in the screen settings after the iPhone has completed configuring it. Tap *continue* to continue with the setup.

- Has your iPhone been restored? Tap begin to transfer your computer data to your brand-new iPhone.

- You'll be prompted to ensure your brand-new iPhone has enough charge to avoid the device turning off in the process of downloading applications and information. Tap *OK* to verify this recommendation.

- You would notice a notification show up on your apps to download in the background.

Chapter 3

iPhone 8 Unique Beginners Instructions

We know thousands of individuals just obtained an iPhone 8 when relatives and buddies members upgraded to one of Apple's newer models, so if you're left with one, here are some iPhone 8/8 Plus changes that may not be familiar to you.

(If you've never used iOS 12 before, then you'll find a lot more improvements, but these improvements will be the ones unique to iPhone 8 compared to previous models - but do take a peek through my other hints for some ideas to get more from your brand-new device).

How to Reboot Your iPhone

If you've used a youthful model iPhone before getting an iPhone 8, then you should know that Apple has changed how you Force Restart the unit.

Using the iPhone 8, the Force Restart procedure is as follows:

- Press and quickly release the *Volume Up* button.

- Immediately press the *Volume Down* button.

- Then press the *Sleep/Wake button* until you start to see the Apple logo.

How to Update the Software

You should upgrade the program whenever a new version comes, but if you have an iPhone 8 (or 8 Plus), you will probably still be in a position to upgrade its software in 2022.

How to utilize it one-handed

This won't take long. Keep your iPhone and double-tap the *Home button* to bring your windows down the display screen (you'll know it when you view it) to make things simpler to reach with your thumb. Double-tap again to move it up. And, if you will be keying in one-handed, reach over and press 'N' contain the emoji button on the keypad, on another web page, you'll find three keyboards, right, middle and left. Choose the best hand indent if you work with your left hands, and the keypad will twist to the left to make it just a little more straightforward to use.

How to charge your iPhone 8 faster

iPhone 8 boasts with a 5-watt charger, but when you can obtain an iPad Pro or USB-C MacBook charger, you can plug your device into those. You'll notice a real improvement in control time when you do. You should strike a 50% charge in thirty minutes utilizing a 29W MacBook charger. You can even charge your device wirelessly using a *Qi charger* (nevertheless, you probably understood that).

How to use the improved Family Portrait Mode

If you've used an iPhone 7, you'll know just a little about Family Portrait Mode, which gets better still in the XS devices but continues to be excellent in 8. Family portrait mode was launched with the iPhone 7 Plus, and an iPhone 8 Plus has got the new capability to enable you to change the light effect you utilize once you take the shot. Just open a Family portrait shot in Photos, tap *Edit,* and use it as an editing effect. Family portrait mode requires (as the name suggests) better family portrait shots. You can even play with different Family Portrait Lighting configurations while taking your shot. (To eliminate the Depth impact, open up the image in Photos in Edit setting and touch the Depth button.)

How to use the Trick cursor

If you are typing or wanting to choose words in editable text, touch, and hang on the keyboard, and you'll suddenly see it has become a cursor to make it much simpler to select words you will need.

Ways to get better Video

Your iPhone 8 catches the video at 4K quality at 30 fps by default. That's excellent quality and should look great, but you can get even higher quality video (though be careful not to fill up your phone with clips you don't need). *Open Settings> Camera> Record Video*, and you may choose to capture your clips at 4K res and a speedy 60fps.

How to handle True Tone

iPhone 8 devices were the first ever to provide True Tone displays. These use light sensors to dynamically change the color of the screen to higher match room lighting, so the colors of what you are looking at on-screen appear to be more consistent; this isn't always what you want, so you can turn this feature off in Control Center by long-pressing the iPhone Brightness button and then switching True Tone off (or on). You can also disable it in *Settings> Display & Brightness>* toggle it to off.

How to use Slow Sync

iPhone 8 series devices were the first ever to support Slow Sync, a technology that tries to mitigate the distraction of taking a graphic using the flash and also attempts to lessen that weird effect that makes the original item in your image appear all bleached out while the background to look darker.

This feature functions by slowing the shutter speed while

making the flash moment faster; this implies the backdrop should look brighter, and the adobe flash distraction should be reduced.

The result? Better photos when working with the display, even of moving items. What you ought to do? Nothing at all, it's built-in.

Chapter 4

How to Fix Common iPhone 8 Problems

If you own an iPhone 8, you might come across occasional issues like display screen freezing, problems with contacts, or overheating. Luckily, these common iPhone 8 issues have easy solutions to get your iPhone 8 back again to performing as it will.

How to Fix the most frequent iPhone 8 Problems

- *Soft or Hard Reset your iPhone*: You might sometimes find your iPhone's display either trapped in a scenery orientation or just frozen. Usually, this is solved with a smooth reset, but if it doesn't handle it, get one of these hard reset. After the iPhone restarts, the display screen should be back again to normal.

- *Ensure that your telephone is operating the latest version of iOS*: If it is not, upgrade it immediately, as a revise may contain necessary software and bug fixes.

- *Update apps*: One of the most frustrating mistakes that can occur when working with your iPhone is having an application quit in the middle of an important task. Check the App Store and install any improvements for the application involved; try uninstalling and reinstalling the application to find out if it begins working again. You can even try contacting the application programmer to see if they're aware of the problem.

- *Reset Bluetooth*: Bluetooth loudspeakers and earphones are something essential for iPhone 8 users because the device does not have a 3.5mm headphone jack port. However, there were some issues reported in linking wireless earphones and other Bluetooth devices. If you still have issues hooking up with a specific Bluetooth device, you may want to try syncing a different device.

- *Reconnect to Wi-Fi or refresh your network configurations:* Sometimes iPhone 8 users statement Wi-Fi issues, including sluggish rates of speed, erroneously getting a "wrong security password" message, or difficulty linking to a network whatsoever. Ensure your web connection and router are fired up and working properly, as well.

- One of the most commonly reported problems with the iPhone 8 has been these devices overheating while utilizing a demanding program or game. Thankfully, you'll find so many ways to handle this particular concern, from disabling certain background features, to eliminating the situation by deleting battery-intensive apps.

- Avoid departing your iPhone in sunlight or close to any heating system elements, like heaters or computer vents.

- If you experience problems with 3D Touch shortcuts showing up or moving prematurely that you should access, you can optimize the 3D Touch level of sensitivity as needed.

- *Reset All Settings:* While this may cause you to reduce any preserved Wi-Fi passwords, it can benefit to fix various problems. To get this done, tap *Configurations > General > Reset > Reset All Configurations.*

- Make certain Apple services will work by heading to Apple's website and looking into the status. If you suddenly end up unable to hook up to the Apple App Store on your iPhone, this is the very first thing you should check. Change your iPhone's LTE settings to Data Only. In case your iPhone phone calls are filled up with static, and there is certainly difficulty making out what your partner is saying, faucet Configurations > Cellular Data > Cellular Data Options > Enable LTE > Data Only. Change LTE back on after looking at your connection quality, if needed.

40 Amazing iPhone Tips & Tricks

Inside the iPhone lies an array of hidden features you might not have even known were around. We've selected our favorite time-saving, life-enhancing guidelines for every model of iPhone, Apple wants to show how exactly easy its products are to use, and the iPhone exemplifies that viewpoint more, perhaps than every other.

This chapter is about taking another step with your iPhone and discovering everything it can do that you didn't find out about. From advanced security to electric battery management and custom notifications, they are our methods for iPhone users.

1. Increase a slow iPhone

Computing devices have a tendency to decelerate as time passes, as components degrade, storage fill with old documents and overlooked/unused apps, and new software is increasingly created for more modern and faster processors.

You can defer the inevitable by following some simple guidelines, including:

- Every once in a while, you should power off your device completely; this clears out the memory space.

- It's also advisable to enter the habit of deleting applications and files you do not use (photos are a common problem for storage space) and archive the latter in the cloud and local backup.

- It's also well worth going right through the configurations and checking which application refreshes in the background, thereby burning up precious control power.

- Upgrade iOS on your device.

Remember that updating iOS has historically been a combined blessing in regards to accelerating your iPhone, but with iOS 13, it has changed.

iOS 13 is especially centered on performance. Apple stated it could make old devices faster, and inside our tests, it seems to have done so.

More tips are available on How to increase a slow iPhone

in this book and other books by Engolee Publishing House.

2. *Start Dark Mode*

If your iOS 13 on your iPhone (at the time of writing, it's available as a general public beta; it'll launch standard in Sept 2019), you can change on the system-wide Dark Setting very quickly. Thus giving all the pre-installed applications and any third-party applications that have built-in compatibility a dark or dark-grey background that's more calming to read at night.

To carefully turn on Dark Setting, open up the Settings application, and tap Screen & Brightness. Near the top of the next display, you will see Light and Dark options hand and hand - tap the main one you want to use. You can even set Dark Setting to seriously automatically at times, such as from dusk until dawn.

If you haven't yet upgraded to iOS 13, you may still find some workarounds. You can test Invert Colours setting, Low Light setting, or Night Change; each one of these offers a few of the advantages of Dark Setting and learning much more inside our dedicated article How exactly to use Dark Setting on iPhone.

3. *Improve your passcode security*

You can unlock your iPhone with your fingerprint or face, depending on which model you have; however, your iPhone is secure if nobody can think of your passcode. If it's as simple as 1234, you're requesting trouble.

iOS now prompts users to make a six-digit passcode rather than the four-digit passcode (here's how to carefully turn a six-digit passcode back to four digits), but there's a more advanced way to make your iOS device better: using an alphanumeric passcode; this means that you may use both characters and numbers in your password, providing you an almost unlimited variety of possible passwords, instead of the roughly 1,000,000 possible six-digit passcodes that could be hacked with the right equipment.

It's simple enough to improve your passcode for an alphanumeric one:

- Open up the *Settings app*.

- Tap *'Touch Identification and Passcode'* (or 'Face Identification and Passcode' on X-series iPhones), then Change Passcode.

- When prompted to enter a new passcode, tap *'Passcode Options'* and choose *'Custom Alphanumeric Code.'*

- Now enter your brand-new passcode. Make certain it's one you can keep in mind.

- Here's choosing a good security password.

- Gleam a new way of securing your iPhone in iOS 12.

- This security change means nobody can plug a tool into the iPhone so that they can hack involved with it. It kicks one hour after your iPhone was locked (if you don't deselect the placing).

- You'll find the environment in Configurations > Touch Identification & Passcode.

- Scroll right down to Allow Gain access to When Locked section, and you'll see USB Accessories.

- Ensure that it's deselected if you don't want devices to have an admission.

- Create custom iMessages for phone calls you can't answer.

- Create custom iMessages for phone calls you can't answer

Sometimes it isn't the right time for a phone call; even though you could just allow phone calls you do not want to consider going to voicemail, sometimes you want to clarify why you are not picking right up. iOS enables you to react to a call with a text quickly.

Based on which version of iOS you're operating, you either swipe upwards on the phone icon that appears next to the uncover slider and choose to Respond with Text message or touch the button labeled Message above the Slip To Answer slider.

By default, you'll receive three pre-written options

("Sorry, I cannot chat right now," "I'm on my way" and "MAY I call you later?"), plus a button that enables you to enter text message there and then.

However, you can customize the instant messages:

Head to Settings > Phone > Respond with Text message.

You can't have significantly more than three responses; however: if you would like to add a fresh one, you need to sacrifice one of the existing options. Tap the main one you're prepared to reduce and enter the new response.

4. *Join an organization FaceTime call*

This feature wasn't ready with time for the decontrol of iOS 13, but soon you'll be able to partake in an organization FaceTime call with up to 32 participants.

To produce a group FaceTime video call, you have to enter several contacts into the address package when initiating the talk.

The interface is just a little different: the tiles showing each participant (there may be up to 32) vary in proportions and prominence depending on how recently it sees your face spoke.

Double-tapping a tile brings to see your face to leading in your view.

You can even launch an organization FaceTime call from within Text messages if a thread gets particularly beyond control.

5. Skip phone calls with Remind Me personally Later

On the other hand, you can get iOS to remind you to call back later. Much like the auto-replies, how you do this depends on your version of iOS: probably, you tap the *Remind Me button* above the glide, but in previous versions, you'd to swipe up-wards before you could go for **Remind Me Later**.

You can prefer to get reminded within an hour, 'When I Leave' or (where applicable) *'When I Get Home.'* Ensure that your address details are current in Contacts, which means that your iPhone understands where home is. The timings depend on your GPS navigation movements.

6. *Create custom ringtones and alert shades in iTunes*

You can create ringtones for your iPhone predicated on any music monitor in your iTunes collection. We viewed this comprehensive here, but last but not least: produce a brief, sub-30-second duplicate version of the monitor; convert the document kind of this monitor from .m4a to .m4r; re-import the monitor to iTunes as a ringtone; sync the ringtone with your iPhone.

On top of that, you can create unique custom iPhone ringtones from your audio creations, which is particularly user-friendly if you undertake the creative focus on the iPhone itself. Produce a 30-second monitor in GB and; go directly to the Talk about options and choose Ringtone; then, assign it to a contact or notification.

7. *How to place custom vibrations on your iPhone*

Wish to know who's getting in touch with you without taking your phone away from your pocket? That's easy - assign a ringtone to a contact. But how about carrying it out all silently? You can not only assign a custom ringtone or text message firmness to a connection, you can also provide them with a custom vibration design.

- Open up Phone or Connections.

- Decide on contact.

- Touch the *Edit button* at the top-right part.

- Scroll right down to find the ringtone field; below, it is a vibration field.

- Tap *Vibration,* and you will see a variety of built-in vibration patterns you can choose from.

- Further down is the capability to put in a custom design: touch *Create New Vibration*, and you will tap on the display screen to generate your tempo.

- If you are satisfied (touch the Play button to see what it'll feel just like), tap Save to create the pattern.

- If that's insufficient, get back to the contact and also assign a custom vibration design for texts.

8. Customize the Control Centre

It was quite a while coming; however, in iOS 13 Apple finally allowed us to customize the toggles and options that occur in the Control Centre.

Head to Settings > Control Centre > Customize Settings. The settings that can be seen are listed at the very top, under the Include, touch the red minus indication to eliminate one, or tap and keep to pull them around and change the order.

Available controls that aren't currently included are the following, under the heading More Controls. Touch the green plus indication to include one.

9. Customize your Emoji

Owners of X-series iPhones (the iPhone X, XS, XS Max, and XR) will currently have enjoyed the pleasures of Emoji: the face catch animations you can create and send to your pals.

But did you know, since the start of iOS 13, you've had the opportunity to make Emoji of yours? They are called

Memoji, plus they can appear to be you, or your preferred celebrity, or just about anyone you choose.

When mailing an Emoji, the first stage is to find the dog, robot, poultry, poop, etc. But if you go directly to the far left of the selection pane, you will notice a plus indication with the New Memoji underneath. Touch this, and you'll be strolled through the (many) different customization steps accessible to you.

We address this technique in more depth here: How exactly to produce a custom Memoji.

10. Save Electric Battery with Low Power Mode

Whenever your iPhone drops below 20 percent power, a note will pop-up to warn you of the fact and also to offer to begin Low Power Mode. Nevertheless, you may use this handy setting if you want to make your electric battery last just a little longer.

Change to Low Power Setting by tapping *Settings > Electric battery > Low Power Setting.*

Low Power Setting reduces power usage by turning off lots of iPhone features. For instance, it'll reduce animations, reduce the time before the display darkens, fetch Email less frequently, switch off Hey Siri, and background application refresh; it generally remembers to eke out your electric battery life for just a little longer.

You might not spot the difference (although you might not get an essential email or social media message if you don't look for it). Overall, though, the iPhone works as normal, and the electric battery can last for a lot longer.

If you found this suggestion useful, you could also like our advice on how best to improve iPhone electric battery life.

11. Maximize Electric Battery Life

Talking about eking out more electric battery life, you can examine your battery utilization on your iOS device to find out if your behaviour could improve things.

Apple enables you to see which of your applications are using in the most electric battery on your device.

Head to *Settings > Electric battery.*

Scroll listed below to the section that presents the Last a day, and the final 4 Days.

Here you will see information regarding which applications used the most battery.

Apple offers up Insights and Recommendations to save you electric battery life in the section above; this may include turning down the display screen brightness or allowing auto-lock.

12. Tremble to undo

That one can be considered a little awkward sometimes, but it could be a bit of the lifesaver.

If you have just typed an extended-phrase and accidentally deleted it or made various other catastrophic mistakes, you can provide your iPhone with a tremble to talk about the undo/redo dialogue container.

Just make sure you're securing to your iPhone firmly before you tremble it!

13. Touch top

Just scrolled down an extremely long list in Notes, or worked your weary way through a huge amount of emails? Rather than laboriously scrolling back to the very best, you can leap there immediately by tapping towards the top of the iPhone's display.

We'd rank this tip with the double-space full stop: it's fairly widely known, however for everybody else, it's a game-changer.

And it's not only Records and Mail; touch top generally works in most iPhone apps. Some apps, cleverly, offer an undo upon this function, for those who tap it unintentionally and lose your Home in an extended article. The wonderful Instapaper arises a Go back to Position control, for example - and if the menu pubs have vanished, you have to tap the very best of the display screen double to activate the feature, to begin with.

Experiment to find out if the application you're using offers various other variance on or development of the handy feature.

14. Set up Do Not Disturb mode

Are you using the *Do Not Disturb* feature? It's ideal for insulating you from interruptions where you want to work or get some rest.

"Do Not Disturb" can be activated from the Control Centre; swipe up-wards from underneath of the display, and touch the crescent moon icon.

A matching moon icon will appear in the very best pub of your iPhone display screen. With *Do Not Disturb* triggered, incoming phone calls and notifications will be silenced.

For a far more advanced selection of options, go to *Settings > Do Not Disturb*; this consists of the power (under the label Planned) to create 'silent hours' every day or night time. You can even allow exceptions: people who'll be permitted to contact You despite having this setting activated, and in iOS 13, it's now possible to create *Do Not Disturb* for one-off events, rather than at precisely the same time every day.

To take action, hard press on the crescent moon icon in

the control Centre and choose from your options: For one hour, Until tonight, Until I leave this location.

On the related note, you might be interested to learn how to tell if someone is using Do Not Disturb.

15. Using, Do Not Disturb While Driving

"Do Not Disturb" has some version settings, such as Do Not Disturb During Bedtime in the iOS 13 upgrade. But the most well-known is the version launched in iOS 11 to lessen distractions when travelling. It blocks incoming notifications (nevertheless, you can arrange an automated reply for chosen contacts only such as "I'm generating right now, are certain to get back in a little bit") and blocks calls too unless there is a hands-free package.

Head to *Settings > Do Not Disturb* and then, under *Do Not Disturb While Traveling*, tap **Activate**.

You will see there are three configurations: Automatically (which tries to work through when you're travelling from your motion, and which we wouldn't recommend, given just how many times we've seen this activate on trains), When Linked to Car Bluetooth, and Manually. Choose whichever option fits you.

Get back to the Do Not Disturb web page of Settings, and you will start to see the automated replies on the bottom of the display. Select who you need to get this reply, and edit the reply by tapping Auto-Reply and then tapping the message.

16. Take photos while shooting videos

You're making use of your iPhone to film a magical instant, and you wish you could snap a picture at the same time. Don't stop saving! Just tap the camera button, which shows up onscreen as well as the shutter button as you film.

You are not using the iPhone's actual picture sensor; you are getting the somewhat less impressive video detectors instead. However, the photos should still come out quite nicely.

17. Portrait Lighting

If you an iPhone 8 Plus, an iPhone X, an iPhone XS, XS

Max, iPhone 11, iPhone 11 Pro or iPhone 11 Pro Max you can gain access to a photographic feature called Family portrait Light (the XR has some Family Portrait Lighting features, however, not all). We find Family Portrait Lighting just a little inconsistent, but it will often produce some attractive results with hardly any effort.

Open up the Camera app, and swipe over the bottom revolving menu, so you're in *Family Portrait Mode.*

Just above this label, you will see a hexagonal icon and the label *DAYLIGHT*, which indicates you are about to have a standard *Family Portrait Mode shot*, with the arty **bokeh** background blur.

If you tap the DAYLIGHT icon, however, it'll pop-up slightly, and you will see it's on the circular menu. Swipe across, and you could scroll through the four other available choices: Studio room Light, which brightens in the subject's face and other 'high factors' and is normally the most dependable setting; Contour Light, which darkens the shadows and sometimes produces a good impact, but often makes people look scruffy or unshaven;

and two variations of Stage Light (color and mono), which slice out the subject and place her or him against a dark background.

The Portrait Lights are just a little better in iOS 13, but we still find the mono settings to be a bit unreliable as it pertains to curly hair. Note that you don't need to apply these results while or before taking the shot. Open up any photo which includes the label Family portrait at the very top left, and you will be in a position to apply them retrospectively. Touch Edit, then touch the hexagon icon, and you will be in a position to scroll through your options as above.

A fresh feature on the iPhone 11, iPhone 11 Pro, iPhone XS, and XS Max gives you to adapt the blur after going for a picture. It's permitted by the individual levels in photos. Whenever we get to try the iPhone XS, we'll fill up you in about how it works.

18. Switch path in Panorama mode

You can transform the path of your Panorama picture in the Camera application by tapping the arrow that appears in the centre of the display screen in the Panorama setting.

19. Use your headphones to have a selfie

Selfies continue being extremely popular, as we're sure you've noticed if the quality of your selfies is a problem, try this useful trick.

A right proportion of iPhone owners know that you can activate the camera shutter by pressing one of the volume buttons (volume up or volume down - doesn't matter which) rather than the onscreen button; this will produce less camera tremble.

But a still better option for selfies - and one which is much less well known - is by using the volume button with an attached couple of headphones.

When the camera application is open on your iPhone, you may use the volume button with an attached couple of headphones to have a photo. Not merely will this reduce tremble even more than using the iPhone's volume button, but it additionally means you may take a far more natural-looking picture from further away or have a photo hands-free.

20. Make an iPhone safe for kids

Kids love iPhones, but there are actions you can take to ensure children aren't able to access unsuitable content on the devices.

Head to Settings > General > Restrictions, and you may limit the usage of specified apps, stop in-app buys, and place a long time for appropriate content; all this is protected in How exactly to set up parental controls with an iPhone.

It's also advisable to check out the likelihood of Family Sharing, an attribute which allows you to talk about applications and content in the middle of your family's devices and never have to purchase them more often than once.

The arrival of iOS 13 provides further parental controls utilizing Screen Time, which enables you to set 'allowances' for the use of certain applications or types of app, warnings when time is running out, and finally a block. (They can ask for more time, but you'll get the ultimate decision.)

21. Stop iPhone addiction

Speaking of Display Time, it's a new feature in iOS 13 that will help you be less dependent on your iPhone. To learn the amount of your time you are wasting on your iPhone, go to *Settings > Display Time.*

Here you will see details about how long you utilize each app, how often you viewed your mobile phone, and what applications you spent the most time with. Touch on your device in the very best section to start to see the Display screen Time breakdown. You can try the break down for today, or going back seven days.

You can set Downtime, with only specific applications being available between certain hours, say after 9 pm. You'll get a reminder right before your Downtime begins. You can decide which apps are allowed during Downtime in the Always Allowed section.

It's also possible to create App Limitations (although these limitations reset every day at nighttime). For instance, you could limit your SOCIAL MEDIA apps, which means you can only utilize them for just one hour daily.

You can set a Screen Time security password to use if you want a few moments more.

22. Quickly add symbols

You might have been making use of your iPhone's keyboard for a long time without realizing that it is easier than you considered to add icons to your communications.

Rather than tapping once on the 123 buttons, once on your selected symbol and then once more on the ABC button to return to the traditional keyboard layout, you can do the whole lot in a single gesture.

Tap the 123 buttons, slip your finger to choose the sign you want to place, then release. Once it has been added, your keypad will automatically revert; one tap rather than three: that's some serious time cost savings right there.

Oh, even though we're talking icons: keep your finger on any notice or mark for another or two, and you will see what other (usually related) icons that the button can provide instead. The buck key offers pound, euro, and yen icons, for example. *If you often type words with accents this is also an instant and easy way to see an accented option.*

There are numerous additional symbols hidden inside your keyboard that you might do not have discovered. Experiment!

23.One-handed keyboard

This feature is feasible if you are on iOS 11 or later version.

Head to Settings > General > Keyboards, and tap One-Handed Keypad. Select Left or Right.

iOS's QuickType system-wide keypad is clever at guessing what you're trying to create, and in many situations will auto-correct your clumsily typed screed into something a lot more accurate.

It gets on top of that, however, when you begin customizing it such that it has learned your private favorite shortcuts and abbreviations and the entire phrases you would like it to expand those abbreviations into.

You may decide that "omg" should be converted into "Oh my God," for example. "omw" should become "On my way." Etc.

You can create a personalized shortcut:

- Head to *Settings > General, scroll down, and touch Keyboard.*

- Select Text Alternative, you will see what text message replacements you now have set up.

To add a fresh one, tap the plus indication. Enter the required full term ("MACBOOK-PRO 2020 with Touch pad" might be considered a good one for a technology journalist), the shortened version that you would like to expand into the longer expression ("MBP," say), and touch Save.

24. Never complete a password, address, or account info

If you wish to save time and also reap the benefits of devoid of to memorize passwords or username and passwords, be sure you start auto-fill. It is possible for your iPhone, iPad, even your Mac pc, to enter your name, address, email, contact number, passwords, and more automatically.

Head to Settings > Safari > Autofill.

You'll need to ensure the info you desire to be filled in is correctly entered in your phone in a variety of places - read this short article for help establishing passwords, control cards, titles, and addresses to allow them to be auto-filled on your iPhone.

Finally, in iOS 12 or later, whenever a security code arrives in a text, it'll automatically be accessible as an AutoFill suggestion - and that means you won't have even to open the Messages application to start to see the code.

25. *Get yourself a thesaurus*

There is a thesaurus option in iOS; nevertheless, you

need to allow it. To take action, go to *Configurations > General > Dictionary*. Now Select English British *"Oxford Thesaurus of British"* (or if you are American, the *"Oxford American Writer's Thesaurus"*).

As long as you're here, you can download translations, such as French-English and Spanish-English too. Now decide on a phrase by tapping it.

Choose RESEARCH from your options (you may want to touch on the arrow to uncover extra options). Now you will notice suggestions of option words, as well as the dictionary description.

26. Rich formatting

While it isn't universally supported, you may use the great format in several iOS applications, including Mail, Records, and third-party applications such as WhatsApp, to be sure about the parts of text stick out; but while you can use, it is also effortless to miss.

Just open an application that supports rich formatting, highlight the written text you would like to edit by double-tapping it, and choose the formatting menu, labelled BIU; following that, select your selected effect, and it will be employed to the selected text message.

Touch the arrow to see additional results such as struck-through text messages.

27. Quick-delete in the Calculator app

If you are using the calculator application a lot, you may like this helpful and little-known time-saving technique.

The *Calculator app*, like real-world calculators, does not have a delete button, which may be annoying if you have just typed out an extended number and made a blunder right by the end.

Thankfully you can swipe over the volume in the dark area at the very top - still left or right, no matter - and for every swipe, an individual digit will be taken off the finish of the physique.

28. Stop music with a timer

This is an excellent trick for anybody who enjoys drifting off to sleep with music. The problem with that is it'll be playing when you awaken each day, and you might have just drained the majority of your electric battery along the way. Using the concealed *'Stop Playing' timer*, you can pick how long you want the music to try out for as you drift off to rest.

Open up the *Clock app's Timer tabs*. (You can get just right to this from Control Centre: tap the stylized clock face.) Choose how long you want your timer to last for and then touch *'When Timer Ends.'* Scroll right down to underneath of the menu and choose 'Stop Playing.'

Press start on the timer and then begin taking part in your music from the Music app. When the timer ends, the music will fade to an end. This technique will also work for audiobooks and other press.

In iOS 13 or later version, you have the excess option of searching for a monitor with a lyric - whatever stage it is that is trapped in your mind because you heard it on the air this morning.

Just open the Music application and enter what in the Search field. It will work even though you don't have all that, but the much longer the term you enter, the much more likely it is going to offer you a correct result.

You can even ask Siri the same question without typing anything.

29. Get an iPhone's display to blink when you get a note

If you discover that the vibration or audio that your phone makes when you get a note is not necessarily enough to attract your attention, there's another component that you can include to the alert: light. By heading to *Configurations > General > Convenience* and scrolling right down to the 'Hearing' section, you can change on *'LED Display for Notifications.'*

Now each time you get a notification, the flash next to your iPhone's rear-facing camera will blink.

30. Find words or phrases on the web page

You can find a specific word or expression on a website in Safari on the iPhone. While on the required page, tap the URL/search bar and enter the desired term. You'll see a summary of search results from the net, App Store, etc., but at the bottom of this list, you will see "on this web page," with the number of matches.

Touch it, and you will see that the email address details are highlighted in yellow. Touch the arrows at the bottom of the display to scroll through the situations.

31. Use AirPods as a hearing aid

When you have a set of AirPods, you may use the Live Listen feature in iOS 12 or later version to carefully turn your AirPods into a hearing help.

Head to Settings > Control Centre > Customize Handles.

Touch on Hearing (under More Settings) to include it to your Control Centre. Now when you select this option in control Centre, it'll magnify voices through your AirPods.

We can't wait around to try out this out so that people can spy on what our friends say behind our backs.

32. Save a website to Books

You can turn webpages into PDFs and add them right to your Books app; that is handy if you are reading an extended web record, or mainly if you've found an HTML publication online and want to keep a duplicate of it.

When you touch Share, scroll over the applications to find Copy to Books. Touch it, and the net web page will be converted and put into your reserve collection.

(Note that this program appears only when you have Booked on your iPhone! Unless you can still Save as PDF and add it to your Documents).

33. Change Siri's accent

British speakers have had the opportunity to improve Siri's voice from male to feminine with the decision of 3 accents since iOS 11; iOS 12 added the decision of Irish or South African too.

Head to Settings > Siri & Search > Siri Tone of voice.

Here you can transform an English speaking voice from Male to Female, or change the accent to American,

Australian, British, Irish or South African. Talking about accents, Siri can result in several different dialects for you.

In iOS 13 and later version gained the capability to translate words and phrases into even more languages - there are up to 50 different combinations. We have an ardent article teaching how to translate using Siri.

It ought to be a straightforward case of saying: "Hey Siri, how do you say Good Night time in Spanish," for example.

34. Ask Siri to do mathematics for you

Regardless of how good a mathematician you may be, having Siri readily available to assist with organic and straightforward mathematics questions is always useful.

Open Siri and recite your equation to it. If the volume is complicated, be sure you say it at a somewhat slower speed, so Siri doesn't misunderstand. We found Siri can also properly separate, multiply, subtract and add, along with some slightly more complicated equations.

35. Create shortcuts for common tasks

In iOS 12 and later, you can group jobs and cause them with an individual Siri command. You will have to download the Shortcuts application from the App Store.

Open up the *Siri Shortcuts application* and touch on *Gallery* to visit a gallery of ready-made shortcuts, such as *Calculate Suggestion, Log water, Make PDF, or Remind Me at Home.*

Once you have the application on your iPhone, you will notice recommendations of shortcuts you might like to use when you swipe down on your Home display screen - Shortcuts are available below your Siri Suggestions of applications you might want to use.

Just tap on the suggestion - which is predicated on something you frequently do, such as send an organization text message, and you'll be taken a right to a message.

36. Measure things

The brand new Measure application in iOS 13 can make

it easy to gauge the dimensions of objects. All you have to do is track the edges of the thing and it'll let you know how long they may be.

Open the application, and you'll start to see the option to go the iPhone to start; eventually, a circle can be seen and the choice to add a spot.

The Measure application is also the new home of the particular level app; this level can be utilized if you would like to ensure that bookshelf you're adding is flawlessly level.

The iPhone uses its Gyroscope to look for the level of the height the iPhone is positioned on; you should have the chance to calibrate it on a set surface before evaluating the situation.

37. Enable Nighttime Shift

Night Change dims the white shades of your screen, to make it easier on your eye in low-light conditions. You can routine Night Shift to occur at the same time every day, or you can manually allow it until tomorrow.

You can even adjust the color temperature such that it is pretty much warm.

Head to Settings > Screen & Lighting > Night Change.

38. Have your iPhone read aloud your Texts

If you require or want your iPhone to learn out your text messages, you'll be able to allow Speak Selection.

To begin with, navigate to *Configurations > General > Availability and toggle the choice 'Speak Selection.'*

If you're to long-press on the speech bubble inside your Messages, you'll now find the choice to 'Speak' - the choice is particularly useful if you have an extended text or decide to begin travelling and want to hear the written text while in hands-free setting.

39. See whenever you receive a message

Inside the Messages app, you can swipe forth to the left to expose the time-stamps of every individual message.

Usually, you can see what date with what time the first message was sent; however, to reveal every individual message from then on, you will have to go through the timestamps by swiping quickly; this is beneficial to either know very well what time the last call was received at or even to find out if your friend was lying about arriving promptly!

40. Call from within Messages

If you are chatting via Messages and then decide it might be useful to talk instead, you can merely touch on the icon for the individual you're texting to see options for a sound or FaceTime call. You can begin an organization FaceTime call from an organization Communications chat too - suppose

Chapter 5

23 Essential iPhone Tips and Hacks You Should Know

Sure, there's a lot your trusty iPhone can already do, even if you have not upgraded to the shiny new iPhone 11 Pro Max yet. At a pinch, you could probably serve small canapés off it. But this pocketable package of question isn't only a fairly vessel into the world of internet pleasure and messaging madness.

There are a large number of cool iPhone features hidden under the surface that you almost certainly weren't even alert to - and not only the data that can litter may bring your phone back from a watery death.

They are among the better iPhone hacks you didn't find out about, and just how you will get them.

1. *Charge Your Phone Faster with an Individual Button Press*

Tired of looking forward to your phone to recharge? Well, there's a way to increase the re-juicing process, and it's remarkably simple. Apply Flight Safe setting. By knocking out all of your phone's Wi-Fi-searching, data-draining communication, it requires any risk of straining off your electric battery strength while it's being driven up. Not greatly true, but if you are pressed for time and seeking to take out of the juice, that extra 4% you'll add 30 minutes linked to the mains will make all the difference.

2. *Shave Seconds Off Your Searches*

With regards to learning the footy ratings or proving a spot, getting where you will need to be on the internet is focused on speed and precision, something is missing if you are forced to knock out type-heavy websites. To save time by keeping down the entire stop icon while keying in and out an address to talk about a short-cut group of URL suffixes. From your classics (.com, .co.uk) to the less used (.edu, .ie), there are quick-strike shortcuts for all those.

3. *Discover just what Your Mobile Phone is Aware of*

Somewhat sinisterly, your iPhone is always gathering data for you in the background - whether it is the applications you're using the most, how much data you're churning through, or even, most creepily, what your location is. To see what we should mean, check out

Settings > Personal privacy > Location Services > System Services > Regular Locations. Here you can view not merely where you've been, but how long you've spent in each place.

4. *Replace a Toolbox Essential*

You've probably submitted away the Compass application alongside the Shares and discover Friends applications in a folder entitled *'Crap I cannot delete'*. You should draw it out again, as it offers a key second function that will assist with your DIY responsibilities. Instead, swiping the left in the Compass application brings up a beneficial level - an electronic bubble measure than can check if that shelf is level.

5. *Lock Your Camera's Center Point*

Everybody knows that tapping the display while going for a picture will set the camera's point of concentration, right? Good. Annoyingly though, each time you move the camera after deciding on a centre point, it disappears. Rather than just tapping the display screen, press for another or two until an *'AF Locked'* container pops up. You will twist, change and swing finished around without dropping focus.

6. *Create Custom Vibrations*

Ever wished you could show who's calling simply by how your telephone feels buzzing against your lower-leg? You will: In Connections, select your person of preference and strike *Edit*. Here you will see a Vibration option. Selecting this will provide you with a lot of options, like the **Create New Vibration** tool. Making your bespoke hype is really as simple as tapping the display to the defeat of your decision.

7. *Correct Siri's Pronunciation*

Siri's a little of the smug know-it-all - so there is nothing better than getting in touch with it on its dick ups. Like when it mispronounces individuals' names as an ignorant Brit overseas. So if Siri says something amiss, inform it. Pursuing up a blunder by stating "That isn't how you pronounce..." you will discover Siri requires the right pronunciation that enables you to check it offers things right. Because everybody knows it's Levi-O-sa, not Levi-o-SAR.

8. *Close 3 Apps Simultaneously*

It's not simply pictures and webpages that support multi-finger gestures. You can toss additional digits into unscrambling your iPhone mess too. If you want to shut multiple applications in a rush for totally innocent, not concealing anything, honest reasons - you can pull three fingers through to the multitasking menu to cull the mess quickly; this means your mobile phone should be snappier in double-quick time.

9. *Manage Your Music on the Timer*

Enjoy hearing just little soothing vocals as you drift off to the Land of Nod? Then you're probably all too acquainted with getting up at 3 am for some unwanted music. Unless, of course, you arranged your music to turn off on the timer carefully. In the Clock app, slip along to the Timer options. Hereunder the 'When Time Ends' label, you can replace the security alarm option for a 'Stop Playing' label; this will switch off the music, whether it is through Apple Music or Spotify, when the timer strikes zero.

10. *Have a Photo without coming in contact with Your Phone*

An oldie, but a goodie iPhone hack, is making use of your volume control buttons to fully capture simple, thus keeping your meaty paw blocking the display screen as you try to strike the touchscreen settings. But if you like to be even more taken off your photo-capturing shutter handles, hitting the volume button on a set of compatible, connected earphones will have the same impact.

11. *Save Your Valuable Data Allowance by Restricting App Access*

You're only a third of just halfway through the month, as well as your 2GB data allowance has already been beginning to look just a little extended. You don't need to scale back on your on-the-go Netflix looking. Instead, go for which applications get demoted to the Wi-Fi-only B-list. Head to Configurations > Mobile Data, where you may make the best decisions on application at the same time.

12. *Improve Your Electric Battery Life*

Limelight, Apple's linked quick-access for key data and services, is ideal for offering access immediately to the latest breaking information, sports ratings, and social upgrade. But very much stuff happening in the background can eat your electric battery life whole. If you don't turn off Limelight features for several applications to take out more life per charge, that is. Just go *Configurations* > *General* > *Limelight Search* and limit what's attracting data behind your consent.

13. *Improve Your Transmission by Knowing Where You Can Search For It*

You don't need to go out of initial floor windows trying to find where your iPhone's connection is most beneficial. Type ***3001#12345#*** into the iPhone's dialer and strike call to release the concealed Field Setting tool. This sub-surface menu becomes your pub chart-based signal indication into an even more simple numerical-based sign signifier. Got a rating of -50? Then you will be enjoying Hd-video streams on the road. Down around -120, though, and you will battle to send a textual content. Just follow the figures to better indicators.

14. *Find out Just How Long You've been Looking Forward To A Reply*

We've all been there: endlessly rechecking our cell phones for a textual content reply, thinking how long it has been since we sent our message of love. There's a simple way to learn, though swipe in from the right-hand part of the display when in a messaging thread, showing exact delivery times for each message delivered and received. True, it isn't as morale-beating as WhatsApp's blue ticks, but it'll still offer you a complicated over why it's overtaking 42 minutes for your other fifty percent to reply. Do affairs take that long?

15. *Share Your Loved Ones Tree with Siri*

Does discussing your parents by their given name cause you to feel awkward? Then train Siri to learn whom you're chatting with. Ask Siri to call your father, and the digital PA should ask who your dad is. Once a contact has been designated to the parental moniker, each time you require pops continue, you'll be supported by simple, fuss-free phoning.

Chapter 6

iPhone 8 - Top 20 Guidelines to Know

To enable you to make the most of the iPhone 8, we've listed twenty full proof guidelines below; this can help you know the iPhone 8 new function. A few of these tips were derive from gossips and speculations that are associated with iPhone 8 plus; they might somewhat differ after release due to upgrade in iOS version and other related improvements. Nevertheless, it will always be preferable to prepare yourself beforehand. Continue reading and understand how to use iPhone 8, just like a pro.

1. *A revamped design*

This iPhone 8 new function is presently the talk of the city. Based on the speculations, Apple will be revamping the whole appearance and feel of (red) iPhone 8 with a curved screen; this might make it the first iPhone to have a curved screen truly. Furthermore, the personal home button may also be removed from your body and would be changed by an ID.

2. *Prioritize your downloads*

Will it ever eventually help you if you are installing multiple applications and desire to prioritize them? The brand new iOS can make it happen very quickly. This feature will surely enable you to make the most of the iPhone 8. While downloading multiple apps, long-press the 3D Touch Identification on your device; this will open up the next menu. Here, you can touch on the "Prioritize Downloads" option to customize.

3. *Rearrange how you share your articles*

That is one of the most uncommon iPhone 8 tips that people are sure you won't be aware of. Whenever you share a sheet or any other kind of content, you get various options on the screen. Ideally, users need to scroll to select their preferred choice. You can customize this with a simple drag and drop. All you got to do is long-press the option and drag it to rearrange your shortcuts.

4. *Drag sketches in your message*

The feature was initially introduced for Apple Watch, but soon became an integral part of the iOS 10 version. We also expect it to be there on iPhone 8 as well. To add sketches in your message, open up the app as though drafting a note faucet on the sketch icon (center with two fingertips); this will open up a new user interface that can be used to drag sketches. You can either make a brand new sketch or drag something on an existing image, as well.

5. *Change the capturing path in Panoramas*

That is one of the most crucial iPhone 8 methods for all the camera lovers out there. A lot of the time, we believe that panoramas feature a set shooting path (i.e., from left to right); this may surprise you; nevertheless, you can transform the shooting path with an individual tap. Just open up your camera and enter its panorama setting. Now, touch on the arrow to be able to change the shooting path.

6. *Pressure delicate display*

This iPhone 8 new function can make the new device a significant stunner. The OLED screen is likely to be pressure sensitive. Not merely will it give a brighter and broader look at an angle, but it'll make the touch more delicate. We noticed a pressure delicate screen in Galaxy S8, and Apple is likely to redefine it in its new flagship phone as well.

7. *Seek out words while browsing*

This trick will surely let you save your valuable time and efforts. After starting any web page on Safari, you can easily visit a term without starting another tab. Just choose the word that you intend to search; this will open up a URL bar at the bottom of the record. Here, don't faucet on "Go." Just scroll down just a little to check out the option to find the phrase.

8. *Add shortcuts for Emojis*

Who doesn't love Emojis, right? In the end, they will be the new way of communication; this may surprise you; nevertheless, you can post Emojis with a shortcut as well. To get this done, visit your phone's Configurations and go to *General* > *Keypad* > *Keyboards* > *Add New Keypad* > *Emoji*. After adding the Emoji keypad, go to *General* > *Keypad* > *Add New Shortcut*, to place an Emoji instead of a term as a shortcut.

Save your valuable settings and leave. Afterward, each time you will write the term, it'll automatically be turned to the provided Emoji.

9. Ask for arbitrary passwords from Siri

We can't list away iPhone 8 tips without including a few Siri tricks. If you want to make a new and secure security password, but can't think of anything, you'll be able to take the help of Siri. Just start Siri and say "Random Security password." Siri provides an array of alphanumeric passwords. Furthermore, you can restrict the number of character types in the security password (for example, "Random security password 16 digits").

10. Adjust the flashlight

This fancy feature enables you to make the majority of the iPhone 8, once you are at night. If needed, you can change the strength of your torch regarding your environment. To get this done, go to the Control Center and force touch on the torch option; this provides the following display you can use to modify the strength of the light. You can even push touch other symbols here to get added options.

11. *Cellular and Photovoltaic charger*

This is only speculation, but if it happens to be true, then Apple would have the ability to change the overall game in the smartphone industry. Not merely is iPhone 8 likely to be charged wirelessly; however, the rumor has it that it will have a photovoltaic charging plate. It might be the first device of its kind that might be in a position to charge its electric battery from an inbuilt photovoltaic plate. Now, most of us need to hold back for a couple of months to learn how a lot of this speculation would be true.

12. *Create new vibrations*

If you want to understand how to use iPhone 8, such as a pro, you'll be able to begin by customizing just how it vibrates. Doing that is fairly easy. You can set personalized vibrations for your connections. Decide on contact and touch on the *Edit* option. In the Vibration section, tap on the *"Create New Vibration"* option; this will open up a new tool that enables you to customize vibrations.

13. *Right Siri's pronunciation*

Exactly like humans, Siri can provide the incorrect pronunciation of the word (mainly names). You can teach Siri the right pronunciation simply by stating, *"That's not how you pronounce <the phrase>."* It'll request you to pronounce it properly and can register it for future use.

14. *Utilize the camera's depth of field*

According to the ongoing rumors, iPhone 8 should come with a new and advanced 16 MP camera. It'll enable you to click exceptional pictures. With it, you can also catch the entire depth of the scene. To get this done, start the Portrait setting in your camera and have an up-close of your scene at the mercy of catch the depth of field.

15. *Established music on a timer*

While working out or going for a nap, lots of individuals start music in the backdrop. Though, this iPhone 8 new function enables you to play music on a timer as well. To get this done, visit the *Clock > Timer option.* From here, under the *"when the timer ends"* feature, start the security alarm for the choice of "Stop using." Whenever the timer strikes zero, it'll automatically switch off your music.

16. *Waterproof and dustproof*

The brand new iPhone is likely to take the waterproof feature of its predecessor to a new level. The device will be dustproof, allowing you to utilize it with no trouble. Also, if by the incident, you drop it in water, then it won't cause any damage to your phone. According to the experts, the new iPhone 8 can stay underwater for as long as 30 minutes; this will certainly let you make the majority of the iPhone 8 with no trouble.

17. *Lock the camera zoom lens (and focus)*

While saving a video, the dynamic zoom compromises with the entire quality of the video. Don't worry! With this iPhone 8 new function, you can lock the zoom feature very quickly. Just go to the *"Record Video"* tab in the Camera settings and turn on the option for *"lock camera lens."* This will set a specific zoom during your recordings.

18. *Another stereo speaker*

Yes! You have read it right; to supply an excellent surround-sound to its users, these devices are likely to have another speaker. Not only through wireless earphones, but you can also pay attention to your favorite tunes on the supplementary stereo system speakers of your new device, as well.

19. *Increase to wake feature*

To save enough time for its users, Apple has produced this phenomenal feature. It can do precisely what it appears like. Whenever you improve the telephone, it automatically wakes it up. Nevertheless, if you want to change this feature, then you can visit your phone's *Settings > Display & Brightness* and turn the feature on or off.

20. *Touch Identification on the OLED screen*

If you want to understand how to use the iPhone 8 efficiently, then you should know how to use the unit. A new consumer might get puzzled while unlocking these devices. It is expected that iPhone 8 will have an impression ID (fingerprint scanning device) directly on the OLED display screen. The optical fingerprint scanning device would be the first one of its kind.

Advance iPhone 8 Tips and Tricks

1. Make the majority of your iPhone 8

The iPhone 8 and 8 Plus might not seem everything the same as 2016's iPhone 7 and 7 Plus, especially with the radically new iPhone 11 Pro max grabbing all the interest. But Apple does make some quite significant changes to its other mobile phones, from improved digital cameras to the capability to charge your brand-new phones wirelessly. Toss in iOS 11, and most of its new features, as well as your phone has a lot of newfound features. Here is a guide to all or any of the features you should explore to discover precisely what the iPhone 8 can do.

2. Transfer data to your brand-new iPhone

Before migrating to the iPhone 8, ensure that your previous phone is working iOS 11. Allowing you to take benefit of Apple's new Quick Set up feature. To kick it off, point your old iPhone's camera at the new model. Both devices will connect, and once you enter your old phone's passcode on your brand-new phone, there's an instant data transfer. The effect: less time inputting old passwords and establishing Apple IDs.

3. Send Money to a friend

You should use *Apple Pay* to send money to friends and family directly with the new Apple Pay Cash feature. To send cash, make sure you have Apple Pay set up on your phone. (To avoid credit fees for Apple Pay Cash, hyperlink debit cards to your mobile phone.) Then open up Messages and begin a discussion with the friend you want to send money to. At the bottom of the display, touch the Applications icon (to the still left of the text-entry container), then faucet the Apple Pay logo design. You can either pay or demand to be paid, and everything happens right within Text messages.

4. Control your video resolution

The iPhone 8 and 8 Plus can shoot higher-quality video than previous phones. By default, video is captured at 4K quality at 30 fps, but that isn't the utmost quality level: you can go entirely up to 4K at 60 fps if you'd like. (You need to be aware that it'll take up a great deal of space on your device.) You can even decrease to a film-like 24 fps, or drop back again to 1080p or 720p firing to save space for storage. To adapt this setting, go directly to the Camera portion of the Configurations app and touch on Record Video.

5. Ask Siri to try out some Music

Exactly like Siri's podcast-playing ability, Apple's digital associate also offers DJ skills. If you're an Apple Music customer, ask Siri to play your music in a genre or even to play some music you prefer. You can add songs to the music queue via Siri, too. Siri will also tell you information about the current song, including (for some content) who plays on the album and when it was released.

6. Find iCloud settings

In iOS 11, a lot of settings you're used to, have moved to new locations. The most dramatic change is that all of your private information - including iCloud-related settings, iTunes and App Store settings, and all of your Apple ID information - all reside in a fresh item towards the top of the Settings app. You can miss it if you're not looking for it. If you need to change your iCloud backup settings or change what iTunes content gets automatically downloaded, it all lives under that menu, which displays your picture and name.

7. Record a video of what's on your screen

Display recording is new in iOS 11. To gain access to it, you will need to visit the Control Middle portion of the Configurations app, touch Customize Handles, and add Display screen Documenting to your set of included items. To start documenting, swipe to uncover Control Middle and touch the documenting icon. You'll receive a three-second countdown, and the documenting will start. The status club near the top of the display will switch red as long as you're recording. To complete recording, faucet the red position bar or recreate Control Center and touch the documenting icon there.

8. Get directions inside the shopping mall (no directory site required)

Apple Maps in iOS 11 gives new shopping-mall and airport terminal maps, and that means you can navigate right to that Chess Ruler store without consulting with a directory site. Maps also now offer street routing features, reducing the opportunity that you will need to slice into the converted street at the last second.

Chapter 7

Top Best iPhones Model Tips
Keyboard Tips

- <u>*Go one-handed*</u>: The QuickType keypad enables you to type one-handed, which is fantastic on the larger devices. Press and contain the little emoji icon and choose either the *left or right-sided keypad*; it shrinks the keypad and brings it to one part of the screen. Get back to full size by tapping the tiny arrow.

- <u>*Pull the plug on one-handed*</u>: if you never want the choice to visit one-handed, check out *Settings > General > Keypad and toggle the "One-handed keypad"* option off.

- *Use your keyboard as a trackpad*: Because the introduction of 3D Touch shows on iPhones, you may use the keyboard area as a trackpad to go the cursor onscreen. It works anywhere there's text message input, and will save you need to try and touch the precise location you want to begin editing. Just hard press anywhere on the keypad and move the cursor around.

- *Picking your Emoji color*: In recent iOS, Apple added lots of new emoji and specifically emoji, which have pores and skin tones. To gain access to them, go directly to the emoji keypad in any application and long press on the main one you want to use. If it has options, they'll show.

- *Adding third-party keyboards*: Set up the application (*SwiftKey or Gboard* are an example) and follow the instructions in the app. Sooner or later, it will request you to go to *Configurations > General > Keypad > Keyboards* and add the third-party keypad.

- *Being able to access additional keyboards beyond Emoji*: When you have more than three keyboards installed, the keyboard will show a globe icon next to the spacebar; virtually any app which has a keypad touch on that world icon and on the other hand to reveal another keypad you have installed.

- *Hiding or teaching auto recommendations on QuickType keypad*: The brand new Apple keypad shows word recommendations predicated on what you type. Unless you utilize this, you can conceal it to offer more space on display. Softly press and keep near the top of the auto-suggest pub and pull it towards the very best row of secrets. You may bring it back by dragging up from the very best of the keypad if you change your brain.

- *Disable keyboard capitalization*: Until iOS 9, whether you handled the shift key or not, all the letters on the keyboard were capitalized. Now, the keypad shows the characters in lowercase when change is off. But unless you want this, you can disable it by heading to *Configurations > Availability> Keypad* and toggling from the screen lowercase Secrets option.

- *Disable keyboard animations*: Apple's keyboard has a pop-up character animation that serves as feedback when you tap the secrets. You can shut it off (*Configurations> General> Key pad> Personality Preview*).

- *Text message replacement shortcuts*: As in every earlier year, one of iOS' most readily useful keyboard solutions is creating shortcodes that become full words or phrases. Head to *Configurations > General > Keypad > Text Alternative*. We think it is beneficial to have one for an address that fills in automatically if we misspell "addresses," adding a supplementary "s" by the end.

Maps Tips

- <u>How to manage preferred transport in Apple Maps</u>: If you discover you merely ever use Apple Maps when walking, you can place the preferred transportation type to be that. To improve it between Traveling, Walking, and General public Transportation, go to *Configurations > Maps* and select the one you want.

- *Us ARKit in FlyOver*: A couple of years ago, Apple developed its Maps app, filled with Flyover, digital 3D variations of major towns. You will shop around 3D metropolitan areas by merely moving your iPhone. Visit a major city - like London or NY - then tap the *"FlyOver"* option. Then all you have to do is move your device and show you around the town.

- *Use interior maps*: Now, you can use inside mapping to stay on course around major department stores. It's limited for the present time; nevertheless, you can check it out in AIRPORT TERMINAL. To use in Home maps, visit a backed location and pinch-to-zoom in before outdoor areas go dark gray. You will see inside the building.

- *Move between building levels on indoor maps*: Once you're in the building map, you will see lots in the right aspect of the display screen. Touch it, and then choose a floor level.

Apple Music Tips

- *How to cover Apple Music*: You can completely cover Apple's Apple Music service, to take action, go to Configurations > Music, and then toggle off Show Apple Music. Now when you attend the application, you are only going to see your music, as opposed to the music on the service.

- *How to gain access to your complete music collection*: To find out all the tunes, albums, and playlists that you added from the Apple Music catalog, as well as any music that you purchased from iTunes, including CDs that you ripped, touch the Library tabs from the app's menu club along underneath.

- *How exactly to edit your Collection categories*: To completely clean up your collection and specify which categories you'd prefer to see instantly, such as styles, artists, or track, tap the Edit button in the very best right of the Collection display, and then toggle on/off your requirements.

- *Where to find your downloaded music*: if you only want to start to see the music that's physically on your device, tap the Library tabs from the app's menu pub underneath the screen, and then tap *Downloaded Music*.

- *How exactly to create a fresh playlist*: Heading on a street trip and want to produce a playlist? It's easy. Touch the Library tabs from the app's menu club along underneath, then touch Playlists, and choose New Playlist. Following that, you can include a playlist name, explanation, music, and toggle on/off whether you want the general playlist public.

- *Where to find Apple's curated playlists*: The "FOR YOU PERSONALLY" tab within the menu pub/bar underneath is a location where you can go to and discover music recommendations hand-selected by the Apple Music team. Recommendations add a curated favorites blend, daily playlists, performers spotlights, and new produce, which focus on you and are customized to your music choices.

- *Where to find top music graphs*: Go directly to the Search tabs in the menu pub along underneath, and then tap "Top Graphs" to visit a regularly updated set of typically the most popular tracks on Apple Music.

- *Where to find top music graphs by genre*: By default, the very best Graphs section in the Search tab teaches you all styles. But you can pick a particular genre, such as Blues, by tapping the All Styles button in the very best right and selecting your genre from the list that shows up.

- *How to gain access to Connect*: Apple has ditched the Connect tabs in iOS 10 (it allowed you to check out performers and curators to be able to see their new products and articles). They have instead buried the feature in the new Search tab. Following that, select Top Graphs, and then scroll to underneath of the display screen to see music on Connect and videos on Connect.

- *Where to find videos*: Apple Music isn't nearly music. It's also about music videos and other video content. Go directly to the Browse tabs in the menu club along underneath, and then touch Videos to see new videos on Apple Music and top music videos.

- <u>Where to find the Beats 1 radio train station</u>: Apple Music offers a 24/7 live-streaming radio place called **Beats 1**. To gain access to it, tap the air tabs in the menu pub along underneath, and then touch the Beats 1 thumbnail.

Where to find r/c: Aside from Beats 1, Apple Music offers channels that derive from genres and various themes. You'll find them under the air tabs in the menu club along underneath. Following that, tap "R/C."

- *How to talk about a record*: Want to talk about a recording via Twitter, Facebook, or wherever? Touch on any record, and then choose the button with the "…" three dots at the very top. Following that, tap Share Recording and choose how you would like to talk about it.

- *How exactly to add a recording to your Play Next queue*: Apple Music can queue up albums you want to hear while on the run. Just add it to your Play Next list. Touch on any record, and then choose the button with the "…" three dots at the very top. Following that, touch "Play Next."

- *How exactly to add a recording to a playlist*: You can include an entire record to a fresh or old playlist. Just tap on the recording, and then choose the button with the "…" three dots at the very top. Following that, tap "Increase a Playlist," and then select which playlist (old or new) you want to include it too.

- *How exactly to download a record to your Collection for offline hearing*: Touch on the recording, and then choose the button with the "…" three dots at the very top. Following that, tap

Increase a Library. You'll then be cut back to the record screen. Touch the button with the "…" three dots again, and then choose the Download option. Oh, and later you will notice the option to eliminate it if you'd like.

- *How exactly to love/dislike a recording*: You can show Apple Music if you value or dislike a record such that it can better tailor music recommendations to you. Touch on any recording, and then choose the button with the "…" three dots. Following that, touch Love or Dislike, depending on your choice.

- *How to produce a train station from a track*: Touch on any music, and then from the music handles menu (tap it along underneath to make it expand into a full screen card) choose the button with the "…" Three dots in the low corner. Following that, tap Create Train station; this will generate a radio train station predicated on that specific tune.

- *How to talk about music*: Want to talk about a record via Twitter, Facebook, or wherever? Touch on any melody, and then from the music settings menu (touch it along underneath to make it broaden into a complete screen credit card), choose the button with the "..." three dots in the low corner. Following that, tap Share Record and then click how you would like to talk about it.

- *How to put in a track to your Play Next queue*: Apple Music can queue up tunes you want to hear while on the run. Just add it to your Play Next list. Touch on any track, and then from the music handles menu (tap it along underneath to make it increase into a complete screen card), choose the button with the "..." three dots in the low corner. Following that, touch "Play Next."

- *How to put in music to a playlist*: Touch on any music, and then from the music settings menu (tap it along underneath to make it expand into a complete screen credit card) choose the button with the "..." three dots in the low corner.

Following that, tap Increase a Playlist and then select which playlist (old or new).

- *How exactly to download a tune to your Collection for offline hearing*: Touch on any tune, and then from the music handles menu (touch it along underneath to make it expand into a complete screen card) choose the button with the "..." three dots in the low corner. Following that, tap Increase a Library. You'll then be cut back to the music control menu. Touch the button with the "..." three dots again, and then choose the Download option. Oh, and later you will notice the option to eliminate it if you'd like.

- *How exactly to love/dislike a melody*: You can show Apple Music if you value or dislike a melody, such that it can better tailor music recommendations to you. Touch on any track, and then from the music settings menu (tap it along underneath to make it broaden into a complete screen credit card), choose the button with the "..." three dots in the low corner. Following that, touch Love or Dislike, depending on your choice.

- *How exactly to see lyrics for a track*: Can't show the actual designer in a track is saying? Browse the lyrics in Apple Music. Touch on any music, and then from the music handles menu (tap it along underneath to make it increase into a complete screen card) choose the button with the "…" three dots in the low corner; following that, tap Lyrics.

- *Switch sound source for music*: Want to improve from your iPhone to a linked speaker? Touch on any tune, and then choose the red arrow button with radio waves (it rests below the volume slider, alongside the button with the "…" three dots. Following that, pick your sound source.

- *Share a musician*: Like tracks and albums, you can talk about a designer with a pal via internet sites and messaging apps. Just touch on any artist's web page (seek out a musician, then click his / her name to gain access to the web page, etc.), then tap the button with the "…" three dots next with their name, and choose Share Artist; following that, pick and choose how you'd prefer to share.

- *How to collection the alarm predicated on when you attend rest*: The Clock application can remind you to visit bed and then wake you up 8 hours later, for example. To create it, go directly to the Bedtime section in the Apple Clock application and arrange it from there.

- *How to routine Night Change mode*: Added in iOS 9.3, Evening Shift is an attribute that can automatically change the colors of your screen to the warmer end of the color spectrum at night. It isn't on by default, so to carefully turn it on, go to Settings > Screen & Lighting > Night Change. Here you arranged when you wish it scheduled to perform or "By hand allow it until tomorrow." You can even establish the "warmness" of the screen from "Less warm" to "More warm."

- *Schedule USUALLY DO NOT Disturb*: If you wish to make sure random electronic mails and

Facebook notifications don't wake you up in the night time, go to Configurations > USUALLY DO NOT Disturb and then toggle the Scheduled option before choosing a period for this to be on.

- _Setup Screen Time_: You can now set limitations on application use as well as observe how enough time you've spent using apps. For many more upon this, check out our complete guide to Screen Time.

Siri Tips

- **Translate**: Siri can translate a small number of dialects into American British (sadly no UK British region support yet). Just ask "Hey Siri, how will you say [Biscuit] in German/Spanish/Italian/Japanese/Chinese language."

- **Hey Siri**: To get Siri working by simply shouting at it rather than pressing a button, go to _Configurations > Siri & Search > Listen for "Hey_

Siri."

- **Disable Proactive Associate**: Unless you want Siri to suggest apps, people, locations, and more by using the new Limelight Search, you can always disable Siri Suggestions (in *Configurations > Siri and Search > Suggestions browsing*).

- **Tell Siri to keep in mind what you observe on display**: Siri can manage reminders, and can also remind you about whatever is shown on your device display screen - whether a website or note. Just say, *"Siri, remind me concerning this,"* and she'll scan the web page and add relevant details to your Reminders app.

- **Ask Siri to fetch a picture for you**: Siri is now able to search your photos predicated on their information and requirements. Ask her to discover a specific picture from 14 July 2019, for example, and she'll do that.

- **Shut up Siri**: Sometimes Siri is merely useful when she isn't speaking. Fortunately, an establishment called Voice Opinions (*Configurations> General> Siri*) enables you to decide when she may use her tone of voice. You are able to toggle the placing to always-on, hands-free only (which works only once using "Hey Siri" or linked to a Bluetooth device), or a fresh ring change option (which halts Siri from speaking whenever your ringer is changed to silent).

Safari Tips

- ***Stop websites monitoring you***: Head to *Settings > Safari* and then toggle the *"Ask Websites never to monitor me"* change to the on position.

- ***Gain access to saved passwords***: Because of iCloud, Safari can store your security password across all of your devices. Head to Configurations > App & Website Passwords then sign in making use of your Touch Identification scanner. Here you can view all the passwords that are saved, and manage them.

- *Find on a Web page in Safari*: To Find text message in a Safari web page, hit the Talk about button on a full page to visit a Find on Web page option (it areas a pop-up on the keyboard).

- *Disable frequently-visited sites in Safari*: Safari displays icons of your most visited websites each time you open up a fresh page. It enables you to delete specific ones by tapping and securing them, however now you can change them off completely by heading to *Configurations > Safari*; following that, *switch off Frequently Visited Sites*.

- *DuckDuckGo*: If you wish to place DuckDuckGo as your default internet search engine over Google, Yahoo, or Bing, go to *Configurations > Safari > INTERNET SEARCH ENGINE* and choose the private friendly internet search engine as the default.

- *Auto suggesting websites*: Like Safari on the desktop, you could have the iPhone or iPad Safari recommend suggested serp's as you type. It's on as default, but unless you want to buy, go to *Settings > Safari > INTERNET SEARCH ENGINE Recommendations* and toggle the feature off.

- *Auto-suggesting apps*: Likewise, as you enter popular app brands into the Safari search Web address box, Apple will attempt and match that with applications you either have or may want. It's on as default, but if you would like to carefully turn if off, go to *Settings > Safari > Safari Recommendations*.

- *Getting the hyperlink quickly*: Settings > Safari > Quick Website Search will determine whether Safari offers up website fits or not for you.

- *Making websites weight faster or conserving your computer data*: Safari preloads the first strike of the search, which helps launch your choice quicker. The downside is that it might use up data. If you wish to transform it off, go to Configurations > Safari > Preload Top Strike and transform it off.

- *Scan your credit card*: Instead of needing to type

all of your details now, you can use the camera to scan your credit cards. With regards to getting into the credit card details either press to car fill up if you already are using that feature with Keychain, or press it and then choose Use Camera on another menu you get.

- **Swipe forward and backward**: Swiping from the display to the display screen from the still left of the display dates back through your surfing background while swiping from the right of Safari moves ahead through your surfing around the background.

Handoff and Continuity Tips

Allowing Handoff between iOS devices: *Head to Total > Handoff* and then toggle the package.

- **Being able to access Handoff apps**: Around the Lock Display press, the application icon underneath the left corner.

- **Allowing SMS mail messages on your Macintosh**:

To get this done, you will need to enable the feature on your iPhone. Be sure you are operating iOS 8.1 or later and then go to *Settings > Text messages > TEXT Forwarding*. Find your Mac pc or iPad you want to permit access and set both devices with a security code. You'll now have the ability to see and send Texts via the desktop.

iCloud Tips

- ***Start iCloud Drive***: Head to *Settings*, touch on your ID at the very top, then go to *iCloud > iCloud Drive*. Here you can control which applications get access to your iCloud Drive and whether they may use Cellular / Mobile Data.

- ***Manage your Storage***: Settings, in that case, your *ID > iCloud > Manage Storage*. From here, you can view how much storage space you have, how much you have gone, and choose to buy more.

- ***Family Posting***: Instead of having your iTunes accounts on all of your family's iPhones and iPads, now you can set up Family Sharing for five people.

Head to Configurations, then tap your ID at the very top and choose the *"Family Writing"* option.

- ***Secure iCloud Keychain Access***: Head to Settings, in that case, your ID at the very *top iCloud > Keychain*, and toggle it on or off.

- ***Send the last location, and that means you will get it even though the phone is lost***: Apple's added an awesome hidden feature that will automatically send the last known location to Apple whenever your electric battery is critically low. Even if the electric battery dies as you've lost the phone behind the trunk of the couch, you can still at least get some idea where it surely got to.

- ***Gain access to iCloud Drive documents***: Go directly to the Documents app then touch "Search" then "locations" before choosing the iCloud Drive option. Here you will see all the documents and data files kept in your iCloud Drive.

Apple Pay Tips

- **_Pre-arm your payment_**: To greatly help speed up your time and effort at the cashier, you can pre-arm your _Apple Pay_ before you get to the counter. To get this done, get into Apple Pay, select the cards you want to use and then keep your finger on the Touch ID sensor. Once complete, you have one minute to use the equipped payment before it becomes off.

- **_Weigh multiple cards_**: There is no limit to the volume of control cards Apple Pay can take, so keep launching them into Finances.

- **_How to gain access to Apple Pay from Lock display screen_**: To gain access to Apple Pay on the Lock display, you can double-tap the _Home button_. Unless you want this feature, you can switch it off by heading to _Configurations > Pocket & Apple Pay and turn off_ "Double-Click _Home Button._"

- **_How exactly to allow Apple Pay Obligations on Macintosh_**: You should use Apple Pay on your iPhone to verify payments on the nearby Mac. To

make sure this is fired up, go to *Configurations >
Budget & Apple Pay and start "Allow Obligations
on Mac pc."*

- ***How exactly to change the default Apple Pay
  credit card***: Head to *Settings > Finances & Apple
  Pay and choose the Default Cards* you want. If
  you just have one card, it'll automatically be the
  default credit card.

- ***Choose an Apple Pay payment cards***: When
  paying with Apple Pay, now you can quickly
  choose which credit card you want to use simply
  by double-clicking the Home button while on the
  lock display screen. It'll talk about all your credit
  cards on your iPhone.

General Tips

- ***Standard or Zoomed screen***: Since iPhone 6 Plus,
  you've had the opportunity to select from two
  quality options. You can transform the display
  establishing from Standard or Zoomed. To change
  between your two - if you have changed your mind

after set up - go to *Configurations > Screen & Lighting > Display Focus and choose Standard or Zoomed.*

- **Set the display brightness**: Either go to Control Centre and adapt the screen brightness slider or go to *Settings > Display & Lighting.*

- **Text message Size and Daring Text**: To improve the default text message size and whether you want all fonts to be strong to help make them simpler to read, go to show & Brightness > Daring Text.

- **10-day forecast in weather**: Head to weather, and on any city swipe up. You now reach start to see the ten-day forecast as well as more information just like a mini weather forecast for your day, sunrise and sunset times, and the opportunity of rain.

- **Select a new wallpaper**: Apple has completely revamped its wallpaper offering for iOS. New wallpapers to be enjoyed in the Configurations > Wallpaper.

- *Reach Wi-Fi configurations quickly with 3D Touch*: If you have an iPhone 6S, 6S Plus, or later, you can drive press on the Settings icon to reveal quick links to Bluetooth, Wi-Fi, and Electric battery configurations; the move helps it to be really quick to leap to the cellular settings.

- *Disable contact photos*: Now, you can toggle contact photos *on or off* on iPhone 6 and later. To improve the settings, which is On by default, go to *Configurations > Communications > Show Contact Photos.*

- *Get back to apps*: When you open up a web link or touch a notification when using an app, you will be delivered to a fresh app to be able to view the info in full fine detail. You'll also visit a new "Back to..." button at the very top remaining of the just-opened app, providing you with the chance to tap it and instantly return the application you were utilizing.

- *Monitor your reproductive health*: Medical

application has finally added a Reproductive Health tab, with options for basal body's temperature, cervical mucus quality, menstruation and ovulation calendar, and more.

- *Delete an alarm*: Apple's swipe-to-delete gesture now works in the Clock app. To delete a security alarm, swipe still left on the security alarm.

- *Search in Settings*: The Settings application has a search field at the very top, which may be revealed by pulling down on the Settings menu; utilize it to get the switches you will need.

- *Enable Low-Power Mode*: The brand new Low Power Mode (Settings > battery) enables you to reduce power consumption. The feature disables or reduces background application refresh, auto-downloads, email fetch, and more (when allowed). You can change it on at any point, or you are prompted to carefully turn it on at the 20% and 10% notification markers. You can even put in control to regulate Centre, and get access to it quickly by swiping up to gain access to CC and tapping on the electric battery icon.

- *Find electric battery guzzling apps*: iOS specifically lets you know which apps are employing the most juice. Head to Configurations > Electric battery and then scroll right down to the new section that provides you with an in-depth look at all of your battery-guzzling apps.

- *Make use of a six-digit passcode*: Apple has always given you the opportunity to established a four-digit passcode, however, now it includes a six-number option, indicating hackers will have a 1 in 1 million Potential for breaking it, rather than 1 in 10,000. Just go to *Configurations > Touch ID & Passcode > Change Passcode*, and then choose "Passcode Options".

- *Change how your display screen responds to taps*: A fresh section under Ease of access in Settings enables you to change how your display responds to taps. You can show your iPhone to ignore repeated details. You can even boost the duration of taps before recognized, plus much more.

- ***Check your battery via the battery widget***: Inside the widgets in today's view, some cards enable you to start to see the battery life lasting longer on your iPhone, Apple Watch, and W1 chip-equipped headphones. Unless you such as this widget, touch the Edit button at the bottom of the display screen and then tap the delete button.

Chapter 8

5 Ways of Fixing iPhone Screenshots Problem

Going for a screenshot on your iPhone is usually quick and painless, with the technique varying predicated on your unique model. On previous versions that have a Home button, it's only a matter of pressing that and the on/off button concurrently. When you have an iPhone 11, iPhone 11 Pro, iPhone 11 Pro Max, iPhone X, XS, XS Max, or XR, then you will have to press the medial side button and 'volume up' at the same time to fully capture the subject of your display.

Reason behind iPhone Screenshot Problems

Sometimes things aren't working needlessly to say, and the typical method for going for a screenshot simply isn't doing the secret; perhaps one of your control keys is stuck, or possibly there's another problem with your device avoiding what is said to be basic features from working. Don't fret, as our troubleshooting guide below will walk you through some option options for snapping that iPhone screenshot.

- Find Your Screenshots

Before we dive into fixes or alternatives, maybe the screenshots feature is working. Open up the Photos application and see if indeed they arrive in the Photos section of the Photos app. You can even tap Albums (bottom level of display screen in the Photos app) and swipe until you start to see the Press Types and touch the Screenshots label.

- Start a Forced Reboot of the iPhone

Before proceeding further, you need to force reboot your device and try going for a screenshot once it's powered back on. For older models that have a *Home button*, take the next steps to force a reboot of your iPhone.

Press and hold the Home button down

Next, *press and hold the Rest/Wake button* at the top or

side of your device; don't let go of the *Home button* while carrying this out. After about ten seconds, you'll observe that your screen will turn black. Sustain your hand on both control keys before Apple logo design is displayed, of which point you can release and await the reboot to complete.

For newer models that don't have a Home button, the procedure is slightly different, and it's imperative to check out directions in the precise order.

Press and release the volume down button

Press and hold the Volume button for approximately ten seconds before the screen turns dark. Maintain your hand on this button before Apple logo design is displayed, of which point you can release and await the reboot to complete. After you have forced a reboot, try going for a screenshot once more. If you are still struggling to do so, keep on to another portion of this troubleshooting guide.

Taking Screenshots via the AssistiveTouch Feature

The iPhone's Assistive Touch features were devoted spot to help users with accessibility issues, permitting them to control their device through easier-to-navigate pinches, gestures, swipes, and voice-activated commands. AssistiveTouch can also are available in handy if you are having difficulty taking screenshots through traditional methods. It could be enabled by pursuing these steps.

Touch the Settings icon, situated on your iPhone's Home Display

The iOS Settings interface should now be shown. Choose the General option.

- A screenshot of the iOS Settings interface

- THE OVERALL settings will now appear. Touch Accessibility.

- A screenshot of the iOS General Settings screen

- Some accessibility-related options should now be listed. Scroll down until you find the one tagged AssistiveTouch, within the Conversation section. Select this program.

- On the next display, tap the button accompanying the AssistiveTouch option such that it turns from white to green (off to on).

A screenshot of the iOS AssistiveTouch settings

Next, go for Customize Top Level Menu.

Touch the plus (+) button, located towards underneath the right-hand part of the display screen. A screenshot of the iOS Customize Top Level Menu screen A fresh icon, also an advantage sign will now be put into this screen. Touch this button.

A screenshot of the iOS Customize Top Level Menu screen

A summary of accessibility features should now appear. Scroll down and choose the one tagged Screenshot, making sure they have a blue check tag next to it.

Tap Done, situated in the top right-hand part of the display. You should now visit a Screenshot option put into your Top Level Menu.

A screenshot of the iOS Customize Top Level Menu screen

You'll observe that a grayish circular button is overlaying your iPhone screen. Touch this new button anytime to open up the AssistiveTouch user interface.

A screenshot of the iOS AssistiveTouch interface

The AssistiveTouch button can be moved by dragging and shedding it to a fresh location on the screen when it ever gets on the right path.

To fully capture the items of your display screen, simply tap the Screenshot icon. The brand new image will be instantly preserved to your Camera Move.

Taking Screenshots with 3D Touch

If you're like the majority of people, you almost certainly don't make enough benefit from your iPhone's 3D Touch-enabled features. This pressure-sensitive efficiency gives you to perform everyday jobs quickly, but the technique is focusing on how to result in it properly to fit the bill.

You can also configure 3D Touch to consider screenshots. Remember that AssistiveTouch must be allowed first, which may be done by following steps above. 3D Touch is available with iPhone 6s or later.

- Go back to the AssistiveTouch Settings screen.

- Choose the 3D Touch option, positioned in the CUSTOM Activities section.

A screenshot of the iOS AssistiveTouch Settings screen

A summary of actions that may be linked with 3D Touch should now be shown; choose the one tagged Screenshot, making sure they have a blue check tag next to it. Now you can take screenshots by simply tapping and briefly holding the AssistiveTouch circular button, eliminating a supplementary tap along the way.

Other Options

If you have tried all the above and remain struggling to take screenshots on your iPhone for reasons unknown, you can test one of the next last-resort measures.

Chapter 9

5 Methods to Fix an iPhone That Keeps Shutting Down

Whether we need these to communicate, entertain us, or make sure we awaken on time every day, we rely on our iPhones to work correctly regularly. So an iPhone that keeps shutting off for no apparent reason is a problem.

What can cause an iPhone to keep Shutting Down

There are a variety of things that might lead to this issue, including faulty applications and water damage and mold, but, in almost all cases, the problem is the battery. There are many ways to show for sure that the battery is the problem: the battery health feature included in the iOS, if your iPhone shuts down at 30% electric battery, and an instrument provided by Apple. Many of these options are protected in this specific article.

There are a few easy software actions you can take to

attempt to fix an iPhone that retains shutting off.

- Hard Reset Your iPhone

When you're having troubles like your iPhone arbitrarily shutting off, the first and easiest step to fixing it is almost always restarting the phone. In cases like this, though, you should employ a particular kind of restart, called a *hard reset.* A difficult reset differs from a typical restart since it deeper resets the operating-system and memory space on the phone (but don't be concerned: you will not lose any data). If the reason for the restarts can be an application with a flaw that triggers it to drain the electric battery faster than it will, this may clear the problem. Some tips about what you must do:

1. *The steps differ predicated on what iPhone model you have*:

- With the iPhone 8, iPhone X, and iPhone 11, click and release the volume up button. Click and release the volume down button. Click and contain the Side button.

- On the iPhone 8, hold down the volume down and Side button at the same time.

- On all the iPhone models, hold down the Home button and on/off/side button at the same time.

2. Keep pressing the buttons before the screen moves dark, and the Apple logo design appears.

3. Release the control keys and allow the iPhone to set up like normal.

- Update iPhone OPERATING-SYSTEM

In some instances of the iPhone randomly shutting off, the problem is in the operating system. If the hard reset didn't work and you own a version of the iOS sooner than 13, you should revise to the latest version of the operating system.

How to update iTunes to the latest Version.

If you try those steps as well as your iPhone can't update its OS, follow these steps:

1. Tap *Settings*

2. Tap *Notifications*

3. Tap each application that's outlined in this section and make its *Allow Notifications slider* to off/white.

4. Update the operating-system

5. When the upgrade is complete, and the phone has restarted, repeat steps 1 and 2, and then change notifications back on for every application whose notifications you switched off in step3.

- *Check Your Electric Battery Health (iOS)*

If you're working iOS 13 or more on your iPhone, there is a feature specifically made to help pinpoint issues with your electric battery. Electric battery Health provides two critical information: the utmost charging capacity of your electric battery and exactly how your battery's power has effects on your phone's performance.

To see your phone's Electric Battery Health, follow these steps:

- Tap *Settings.*

- Tap *Battery.*

- Tap *Battery pack Health*

THE utmost Capacity menu shows the full total control capacity your electric battery can hold, the bigger, the better. In case your Maximum Capacity is surprisingly low, that could be an indication of the problem with the electric battery.

The Maximum Performance Ability menu lets you know if the performance of your iPhone has been automatically reduced due to problems with the electric battery. If you see anything apart from Peak Performance Capacity, that could be an indication that your electric battery has issues. The Electric battery Health section will also let you know if your electric battery is at a spot where it requires to be changed.

- *Restore iPhone from Back-up with DFU*

In case your iPhone continues to be shutting down unexpectedly, you are going to need to get one of these bigger steps: a *DFU* restores of your iPhone. DFU, which means **Disk Firmware Upgrade**, creates a brand new installing of all software on the iPhone, not only the operating system, which is a more extensive kind of reset. To get this done, you are going to need a pc with iTunes installed onto it that you can sync your iPhone. Once you have got that, follow these steps:

1. Connect your iPhone to the computer via USB.

2. In iTunes, make a backup of your iPhone by clicking *BACKUP Now* in the primary iTunes window.

3. With this done, you will need to place your iPhone into *DFU Mode*. How you do that depends on the model you have:

For iPhone 8, iPhone X, and iPhone 11, quickly press and release the volume up button, then your volume down button, press and contain the Side button. Keep pressing the medial side button and, when the display turns dark, press and keep volume down. After five seconds, forget about the medial side button, but keep pressing volume down. Whenever your iPhone shows up in iTunes, forget about the button.

For iPhone 8, press and maintain the on/off button and volume down button at the same time. When a window arises in iTunes that says iTunes has recognized an iPhone in a recovery setting, forget about the volume down button. If the iPhone's display is black at this time, you're in *DFU Mode*.

For all the models, the steps will be identical to the iPhone 8, except you press down the on/off and Home buttons rather than the volume down button.

1. Regain your iPhone from the volume up you did in step 2.

- *Contact Apple for battery Replacement*

If none of the other activities you've tried up to now has solved the problem, which may be because the problem has been your iPhone's hardware, not software. Maybe the electric battery in your iPhone is faulty or by the end of its life; this may affect any model of iPhone, but Apple has found a specific problem with some batteries in the iPhone 6S. This has even created an instrument that enables you to check your iPhone's serial volume to see whether it's got that problem. If the website confirms that your iPhone battery has that concern, follow the steps detailed on that web page to obtain a repair.

Even though you don't possess an iPhone 6S, a defective battery or other hardware failures might be the reason for your issue. Apple is your very best bet so that you can get help, so contact the support to get technical support.

How to Group Applications

Creating folders on your iPhone is a sensible way to reduce mess on your home screen. Grouping apps collectively can also make it simpler to use your phone - if all your music applications are in the same place, you would not have to be searching through folders or looking at your mobile phone when you wish to utilize them.

How you create folders isn't immediately apparent, but once you understand the secret, it's simple — some tips about what you should know about how to make a folder on your iPhone.

How to Create Folders and Group Apps on the iPhone

- To make a folder, you will need at least two applications to place into the folder. Determine which two you want to use.

- Gently touch and hold one of the applications until

all applications on the screen start shaking (this is the same process that you utilize to re-arrange apps).

NOTE: Making folders on the iPhone 6S and iPhone 7, the iPhone 8 and iPhone X, and iPhone 11 and 11 Pro, is just a little trickier. That's because the 3D Touchscreen on those models responds differently to different presses on the screen. When you have one particular cell phones, don't press too much or you'll result in a menu or shortcut. Only a light touch and hold will do.

- Pull one of the applications at the top of the other. When the first application appears to merge into the second one, take your finger from the screen. Dropping one form into the other creates the folder.

- What goes on next depends upon what version of the iOS you're working with or using.

- In iOS 7 and higher, the folder and its own recommended name take up the whole screen.

- In iOS 4-6, you Typically the two applications and a name for the folder in a strip over the screen

- Every folder has a name assigned to it by default (more on this in a moment); nevertheless, you can transform that name by touching the x icon to clear the recommended name and then type the name you want.

- If you wish to add more applications to the folder, touch the wallpaper to close the folder. Then pull more apps into the new folder.

- When you've added all the applications you want and edited the name, click on the Home button on the leading Centre of the iPhone as well as your changes would be saved (precisely like when re-arranging icons).

TIPS: *When you have an iPhone X, 11, or newer, there is no Home button to click. Instead, you should tap **Done** on the right part of the screen.*

How Default iPhone Folder Titles Are Suggested

When you initially create a folder, the iPhone assigns a suggested name to it. That name is chosen predicated on the App Store category that the applications in the folder result from; for instance if the applications result from the Video games category, the recommended name of the folder is Video games. You should use the suggested name or add your own using the instructions in steps above.

How to Edit Folders on Your iPhone

If you have already created a folder on your iPhone, you might edit it by changing the name, adding or removing apps, and more. Here's how:

- To edit a pre-existing folder, touch and hold the folder until it starts to move.

- Touch it another time, and the folder will open up, and its material will fill up the screen.

- You may make the next changes

- Edit the folder's name by tapping on the written text.

- Add more applications by dragging them in.

- Remove applications from the folder by dragging them away.

- Click on the Home button or the Done button to save lots of your changes.

How to Remove Apps From Folders on iPhone

If you wish to remove an application from a folder on your iPhone or iPod touch, follow these steps:

- Touch and hold the folder that you would like to eliminate the application from.

- When the applications and folders start wiggling, remove your finger from the screen.

- Touch the folder you want to eliminate the application.

- Drag the application from the folder and onto the

home screen.

- Click on the Home or Done button to save lots of the new set up.

How to Add Folders to the iPhone Dock

The four applications over the bottom of the iPhone reside in what's called the Dock. You can include folders to the dock if you'd like. To achieve that:

- Move one of the applications currently in the dock away by tapping, keeping, and dragging it to the primary section of the home screen.

- Move a folder into space.

- Press the Home or Done button, depending on your iPhone model, to save lots of the change.

How to Delete a Folder on the iPhone

Deleting a folder is comparable to eliminating an app. Some tips about what you must do:

- Pull all the applications from the folder and onto the home screen.

- When you do that, the folder disappears.

- Press the home or Done button to save lots of the change, and you're done.

Chapter 10

iPhone 8 Guidelines: How to unlock its Photographic Potential

Taking photos in the iPhone's default camera application is pretty simple and straightforward - in fact, almost too simple for individuals who need to get a little more creative using their shots. Well, that's all transformed on the iPhone 8, which not only brings a fresh wide-angle zoom lens but a pleasant assisting of new software features that you should explore.

The difficulty is, a few of these aren't immediately apparent, and it's not necessarily clear just how to take benefit of the excess photographic power stored in your shiny new iPhone.

That's why we've come up with this guide for the iPhone digital cameras, to get a solid foothold and springtime towards Instagram greatness. Continue reading and get snapping.

1. *Figure out how to look beyond your frame*

When shooting the typical (26mm comparative) zoom lens, the iPhone use the wide-angle zoom lens showing you what's happening beyond your frame, a little just like a range-finder camera. Those digital cameras have always been popular with professional road photographers because they enable you to nail the precise moment when a fascinating character walks into the frame.

You shouldn't do anything to create this up - endure your iPhone with the camera application open and point it towards the scene to view it in action. Look for a photogenic background like a vacant road, then use the wide-angle preview to time as soon as your subject matter enters the shot. Want to keep the wide-angle view of your picture carefully.

2. *Adjust your compositions*

Here's another fun new feature on the iPhone that's great if you can't quite determine the ultimate way to take a picture. You'll need to go to the main configurations, wherein the Camera section; you'll find an option called "*Composition.*" If you enable "Photos Catch Outside the Framework," the camera will record two photos at the same time - one using the wide-angle zoom lens, and another using the typical angle.

There are always a few facts to consider when working with this nifty trick. First is that you'll have to take in the HEIF format, which isn't always dealt with well by non-iOS devices. Also, the broader position picture will be erased if it's not used within thirty days, so you'll have to be reasonably quick with your editing and enhancing.

To get the wide-angle view of the shot, tap *'Edit'* within

the photo, then your cropping icon, then press the three dots button in the very best right and choose "Use Content Beyond your Frame."

3. *Manage HDR*

The iPhone include Smart HDR, which is started up by default; this automatically detects the light levels in your picture and protect both shows and shadows for a far more balanced image.

More often than not, you will see occasions when challenging conditions lead to a graphic, which is nearly right. If you'd favour less processed photos to edit within an application like Lightroom, check out the configurations menu, find the Camera section, then switch off Smart HDR.

The great thing concerning this is it doesn't eliminate using Smart HDR for several scenes - in the Camera application, you'll now see an HDR button at the very top to turn it On/Off. It just means your default capturing will be without Smart HDR's sometimes overzealous processing.

4. *Reach grips with Night Mode*

Night mode is a new feature for the iPhone and it's something we've been waiting around to see in a while. It's not an ardent setting you can opt for - instead, it'll activate automatically when the iPhone detects that ambient light conditions are on the reduced side.

Nevertheless, you can still have little control over it once it is used; tap the night time setting icon at the left, and you may use a split to choose a faster shutter speed if it's brighter than the telephone realizes, or leave it on Car - or you can also choose to turn it off entirely carefully.

It's worth keeping your iPhone constant on the surface, or perhaps a tripod if you have one, as the telephone will recognize this and raise the shutter rate to 30 mere seconds, which is potentially ideal for night sky photos.

5. *Grasp the ultra-wide-angle lens*

The iPhone will be the first ones with a super wide-angle lens. If you haven't used one before, their 13mm equivalent field of view will come in super-handy for several different subjects, but particularly landscape and architecture, where you want to fit in as much of the scene as possible.

If you wish to exceed dramatic building pictures, one common technique utilized by professional scenery photographers is to juxtapose one close object with a distant object - for example, some close by plants with a long way background subject.

You could also want to use it in a while composing in portrait orientation, for a fascinating new look that wouldn't have been possible before with older iPhones.

6. *Portrait setting is not only for humans*

Even though iPhone XR had a great camera, you couldn't use the inbuilt Family portrait mode for anything apart from human subjects. Bad information for pet-lovers, or merely those who wish to create a shallow depth of field results with any subject.

That's all transformed for the iPhone, which uses its two

digital cameras to help you to take shallow depth-of-field impact images for many different subjects, and has been specially optimised for domestic pets. To begin with, all you have to do is swipe to *Family portrait mode* and point the camera the four-legged friend. It'll tell you if you're too near to the subject and instruct you to move away. The details are nearly perfect, but they're perfect - particularly if you're looking on a little screen.

7. *Locate those lacking settings*

Through the keynote release of the iPhone, it was announced that the native camera application would be simplified to help you consider the key method of shooting your images.

That's great and produces a much cleaner interface, but it can imply that some configurations are now just a little concealed away. If you think where they've eliminated, touch the arrow near the top of the display, and you'll find a range of different alternatives, including aspect percentage, adobe flash, night setting (if it's dark enough), timer and digital filter systems.

8. *Try the new 16:9 aspect ratio*

This is an attribute that is new for the iPhone, adding a new aspect ratio to the prevailing 4:3 and square (1:1) options. Using a 16:9 aspect percentage is ways to get more full shots which ingest more of the scene, and also eventually screen very nicely on the iPhone display screen.

You'll need to activate it from the menu - the default is 4:3. It's well worth also using the 16:9 aspect proportion with the ultra-wide position to get some good great breathtaking type shots.

Chapter 11

How to start Dark Setting on your iPhone in iOS 13

First, check out *'Configurations'* and then look for *'Screen & Lighting.'* Once there, you'll see an all-new interface that places dark setting front side and centre. You will toggle between *'Light'* and *'Dark'* mode with only a tap, assuming you want to activate it manually; however, its implementation within iOS is just a little smarter than either 'on' or 'off.'

Under the two main options, you'll also visit a toggle marked *'Automatic'* which, as you may be able to think, switches dark setting on alone, linked with sunset and sunrise. Additionally, you then have the choice to define specific times for dark settings to allow and disable.

Dark mode has shown to be one of the very most hyped features approaching to cellular devices in 2019. It isn't just a capability destined for iOS 13 either, it's a significant feature in Google android ten plus some devices have previously instigated their own undertake dark setting - cell phones like the Asus ZenFone 6 and the OnePlus 7 Pro.

What does Dark Mode in iOS 13 do?

A part of dark mode's charm originates from the decrease in power usage it brings, particularly on devices that use OLED shows, like the iPhone X, XS, and XS Max. Beyond power intake, however, darker interface shades also lessen eye strain, particularly when being viewed in dark surroundings. In some cases, alternative UI and font colours are also associated with alleviating conditions like Scotopic Level of sensitivity Syndrome - an affliction commonly within people that have dyslexia, which makes text visibility and comprehension difficult.

How to Upgrade Applications on your iPhone in iOS 13

If you're used to manually updating your applications on either an iPhone, iPad or iPod touch by going to the updates tabs in the App Store, then iOS 13 has made some changes.

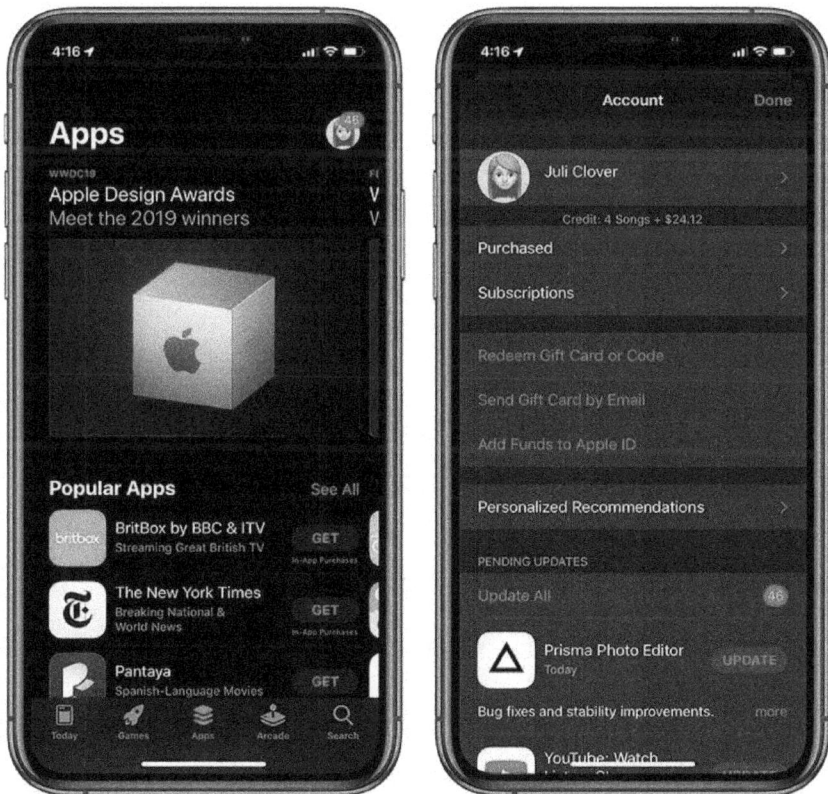

That tabs has eliminated and has been changed by *Arcade*. If you don't anticipate using the new Apple Arcade membership video gaming service, then there's no chance to eliminate this.

Here's how to revise your applications in iOS 13:

- Start the App Store on your iPhone.

- Tap the round consumer icon at the right-hand corner.

- Scroll down, and you'll see a list of all of your applications that either have updates available or have been recently updated.

- If an application comes with an update available, you can hit the button to start it manually

Do applications automatically upgrade in iOS 13?

It appears clear that the reason behind Apple moving this program is because applications tend to update themselves quietly in the background, removing the necessity for anybody to manage application updates manually. The downside with this is that it could be challenging to learn what new features have found its way to applications if you're not looking at the release notes.

Chapter 12

5 Ways of Upgrading Your iPhone Digital Photography for Instagram

1. Minimalism is Key

Our number 1 Instagram photography suggestion is to consider photos that look great and professional with your iPhone; you would need to believe. Why? Because it is not only better - but it's much simpler to choose one new subject matter and make that the centre point of your image.

The sure sign of the amateur is a person who tries to match so many subjects to their imagery. "But my image would be filled with vacant space!" you may protest. That's flawlessly fine. Professional photographers call bare space, *'negative space,'* which is another technique which makes your centre point stand out.

The ultimate way to do this is to go closer to the topic and remove anything in the shot that may distract the viewer.

This can make your Instagram photography appear to be like an expert did it. As you keep up to apply this, you'll come to find that minimalism is the most shared on systems like Instagram, because photos with ONE centre point stick out on smartphone screens.

2. **Get low in Position**

Understandably, your camera move shouldn't be filled with selfies. Just as your camera move shouldn't contain images used at chest elevation.

Among the quickest ways to update your Instagram digital photography and create images that stick out is to take from a lesser position than what you're used to. You don't need to get too low either, capture from less than what you're used to.

When you take your subject or centre point from such a minimal angle that the sky is the only background, what you finish up doing is following both Instagram picture taking tips- making the image extremely attractive on the system like Instagram.

So when you're finally more comfortable with the thought of looking, "extra" according to some people, you'll be able to start squatting and even kneeling to be able to get the best low-angle images.

3. <u>Depth of Field</u>

Precisely what does *"depth of field"* mean? Blurring backgrounds, of course! Everyone knows an image with blur looks a lot more interesting than a graphic where the background and the foreground are both in concentration.

When you Utilize zoom lens accessories to mention a feeling of depth in your images, i.e. Telephoto lenses, you'll be able to attract people's attention - whether you're photographing accessories for Instagram, or just taking scenery photographs.

Besides getting hold of iPhone accessories, a straightforward technique like using "leading lines" that direct the audiences' focus on whatever it is that has been snapped is a superb way to produce depth for your Instagram digital photography. For instance, going for a picture of the road, railway track, a riverbank, fences, and pathways are an excellent leading line!

Once you have found your leads, you can create some depth in the foreground by using found items like stones or leaves or other things, for example, When you absolutely cannot find anything in the foreground that could add a component appealing, then get back to Suggestion #2 and "Get Low in position"! Take from a lesser angle, and you will be amazed what you can catch.

4. Get Up-Close and Personal

Okay, so right now, you've probably determined that each of the tips accumulates from the prior tips so that by enough time you've mastered this whole list, you're practically an expert!

Your Instagram picture taking needs details! It might be hard to trust, but a great deal of iPhone professional photographers make the error of not getting close enough to the centre point. Particularly when they're photographing something with a great deal of fine detail - i.e. When you capture from a long distance, the picture eventually ends up being a little dull and impersonal; however, when you get near to the thing, you all of a sudden have an image that involves life - particularly when you take portraits of others or even your selfies. When you move nearer to the subject, you can properly catch cosmetic features and feelings that would build relationships with the viewer.

Even the newer iPhones remain unable to shoot HQ images of subject matter close up and personal, so our reward Instagram photography suggestion is that you would have to get your hands on the macro zoom lens, like the *TrueLux macro zoom lens*.

What this zoom lens can do is allow your camera to target incredibly near to whatever you're shooting and then add visual interest (and depth) to your photograph, simultaneously.

5. Don't Be Scared of the Silhouette

That one seems just like a no-brainer, but many individuals continue to be afraid to embrace silhouettes on the Instagram grid.

First of all, **what is a silhouette?** *It's mostly when an object's form is captured against a gleaming light. It's not the same thing as a shadow.*

Silhouettes add an air of secret to an image, and against an extremely bright background, a silhouette really can look quite beautiful on your Instagram feed!

Another best part concerning this particular Instagram photography technique is that it is really simple to create images of a silhouette on your iPhone. You just need to know what you want to take a picture of, and then capture towards the light. That's it!

If you'd like to ensure that your subject's silhouette looks unmistakable but still dark, check out your iPhone camera app, tap the screen to create the focus, and then swipe right down to darken the camera exposure - you can still darken the subject even further with photography editing apps.

The optimum time to consider silhouette photographs, despite having your iPhone, is during what professional photographers refer to as the *golden hours of sunrise and sunset.* When sunlight is low coming, then you can position the source of light behind the topic, which means that you'll get a perfectly coloured sky as the background - taking benefit of tips.

You do not necessarily have to hold back for the golden hour to consider silhouette photographs, so long as your source of light is behind the subject.

For instance, if you are shooting indoors, you merely have to put your subject before the window (to consider advantage of daylight), or before a band light/ softbox if daylight is no option.

Chapter 13

17 Surprising Things You didn't Know Your iPhone 8 could do

1. <u>The secret magnifier</u>: Tap your *home button* 3x (times) to carefully turn your phone into handy magnifier - with a slider to regulate the focus and an optional flashlight so you can get nearer to things at night — ideal for reading all the facts, looking at bugs, and digging out pesky splinters.

2. <u>Voicemail transcription</u>: Because of iOS 13, your iPhone 8 will now automatically transcribe your voicemails, and that means you need not bother hearing them (especially annoying whether it's just the audio of someone dangling up). The feature still has a few kinks to iron out, so you may notice the unusual missing phrase, but it's already reasonably workable.

3. <u>Change the brightness of the torch</u>: Already indispensable for looking under cinema seats for

dropped car secrets, the iPhone 8 flashlight is currently fully controllable with 3D Touch. Hard-press the torch icon to see your options - shiny, medium, or low light, depending on how stunning you want it to be.

4. <u>Edit live photos</u>: Live Photos (introduced in iOS 9) enables you to catch a few structures of video around your still images, providing you amazing "moving photos" that appear to be something away of *Harry Potter*. Not used to iOS 10 is the capability to edit your live photos just like some other picture - crop, resize, make lighting modifications, and edit the timing of the live movement.

5. <u>Close all Tabs in Safari</u>: Given that Apple enables you to come with an unlimited number of Safari tabs open up at precisely the same time, it's rather easy to find your iPhone clogged with a massive selection of different home windows. Using the iPhone 8, eliminated are the times of spending a complete evening swiping all of them shut one-by-

one - contain the tabs button in the underneath right-hand corner and choose "close all tabs."

6. <u>Ask Siri to have a selfie</u>: Shout *"have a selfie"* at the iPhone 8, and a couple of things may happen: Siri will automatically activate the front-facing camera, and everyone around you should understand you're going to draw a pouty face. Fortunately, Siri is now able also to operate on the back camera too ("have a picture" or "have a video"), which is particularly handy if you are fumbling for the right button with gloves on.

7. <u>Doodle on your photos</u>: Open up any image in the Photos app, tap the *Edit button*, and then your icon that appears like three dots in a group - providing you the option to include a "markup." It's helpful for things such as circling important details and adding handwritten records to photos, and also for ridiculous stuff like sketching googly eye on your kitty.

8. <u>Handwritten texts</u>: It's likely you have already

discovered that one unintentionally. Convert your phone on its part while you're keying in an iMessage, and it becomes an electronic notepad so that you can finger-write your text message instead of keying in it. Everything you probably skipped though is the excess real estate you can get it done - swipe left to find three extra screenfuls of writing/doodling space.

9. <u>Make your phone display for notifications</u>: Unless you like hearing the ding or feeling the hype, you can make your iPhone 8 blink its torch at you when you get a notification instead. To activate the feature, go directly to the iPhone's configurations menu, check out General and Option of finding the *"LED Adobe flash for Notifications"* option.

10. <u>Find the camera from the lock screen</u>: If you are missing the useful little camera shortcut which used to sit in the lock-screen, don't - it's gone, but it has been replaced with something even easier. Just swipe remaining to open up the camera, assisting you to shoot in the blink of an eye (or

with the swipe of the finger).

11. <u>Hit reset</u>: When you have to reset your iPhone 8 for just about any reason, you may be wondering how you did it that the *Home button* has disappeared. It's just easy, and as unadvertised by Apple - *press down the Power and the volume buttons at the same time until you start to see the Apple logo design.*

12. <u>Sleep better</u>: The majority of us use our mobile phone noisy alarms to get right up each day - but iPhone 8 users can get a much better night's rest than most because of the new Bedtime feature. Instead of merely establishing a wake-up call, Bedtime enables you to choose the number of hours you want to rest - which include an awareness of telling you if it is time to go to bed. The feature can also monitor your sleep design via Apple Health insurance and inform you if you want pretty much of the snooze. Just open up the Clock application and choose Bedtime at the bottom of the screen to begin with.

13. <u>Lock your camera zoom lens</u>: The twin zoom lens camera that is included in the iPhone 8 Plus is one of the biggest reasons to buy it - nevertheless, you might find a celebration when you wish to turn one of these off. Pro users should force a go through the telephoto zoom lens, for example, and videographers should avoid the minor flicker that originates from switching. Go to your Photos & Camera configurations toggle the *"Lock Camera Zoom lens"* option on.

14. <u>Sing along to your favourite songs</u>: The blessing or a curse for whoever you're in the same room with - touch the three-dotted lines underneath the right-hand part of the "Now Taking part in" display in Music to start to see the lyrics to whatever you're hearing. Remember that it presently only works for some songs you've purchased via iTunes.

15. <u>Seek out photos via Siri</u>: Just about everyone having phones filled with pictures iOS 10 will sort them out for all of us - sifting images into years, places, encounters, and "remembrances." Finding

what you are considering can still sometimes be difficult, though, and you may now use Siri to make an effort for you. Ask Siri to "Show photos from August 18", "Show photos from last Mon," "Show me photos from Hong Kong," or even "Show me photos of pet cats" to thin down the search.

16. Quickly browse your unread emails: Apple's Mail application can already help you keep an eye on your emails using its swipe-able flagging system, but it's still easy to get bogged down with unread text messages. On iPhone 8's iOS 13, just faucet the icon underneath the left-hand part of the Email app showing only the email messages you haven't read yet.

17. Remove your annoying apps: Finally, you can be rid of Shares! Hardwired into iPhones for a long time, Apple applications like Shares, Newsstand, Passbook, Compass, and Tips are essential to home screen symbols for some and irritating display screen clutter for others. From iOS 10

onwards, if you would like to eliminate them, touch and keep as usual (and if you change your brain later, you can always download them again from the App Store)

CHAPTER 14

Secret iPhone Camera Features Strange to You

Do you want to make the full use of your iPhone camera when you take photographs? As it's easy to take a photo with your iPhone, the excellent and crucial iPhone digital camera features are hidden from regular iPhone users. So, in this section, you'll find out the concealed iPhone camera features that every iPhone users must use.

- Swipe Left for Swift Access to Your iPhone Camera. How often have you seen or witness an incredible scene in front of your eyes, only to discover that it's gone at the time you're prepared to take a photo? You can improve your possibilities of taking a perfect shot if you know how to use your camera effectively.

- In case your iPhone is locked, you can press the home button to wake up your phone, and then swipe left through the lock display.

- The camera would open immediately, and you won't even need to enter your password to unlock your iPhone. This trick would make you begin capturing in less than a second!

- However, what if you're already making use of the iPhone, and also you want to access the digital camera quickly, swipe up from the lower part of the screen to open the Control Centre as shown below.

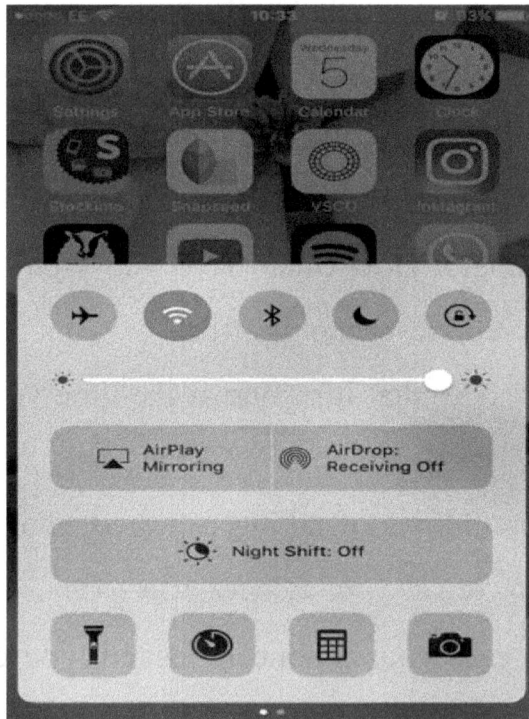

From here, select the camera icon in the bottom right, and you're ready to start taking pictures!

How to Set Focus and Exposure

If you haven't set focus and exposure, the iPhone can do it for you automatically. Usually, it can be a reasonably good job. Furthermore, that's how most iPhone users take almost all their photographs.

There are a few times, though, when autofocus fails - or when you wish to Focus on something in addition to the apparent subject.

That's when you'll want to create focus manually. That is super easy to do - Tap the location on the display where you'd prefer to set Focus, and the camera deals with others.

What distinction does the *focus* make? If you go through the picture above, the Focus is defined on the blossom in the foreground. The topic is bright and shiny, as the bloom petals and leaves in the background are blurred.

When you Tap on the screen to set Focus, the camera automatically sets the exposure. The exposure refers to improving the brightness of an image. So it's essential to get the exposure right if you are taking your picture.

*NB: When you wish to set **Focus**, check out the display to find out if the lighting of the image appears suitable. If it seems too vibrant or too darkish, you can change exposure before taking the picture.*

After you've Tapped on the screen to create focus and exposure, the exposure slider with a sun icon would be observed. Swipe up to help make the picture brighter or right down to make the image darker.

Efficaciously setting focus and exposure is one of the primary element skills that a photographer must master. When it takes merely a few Taps to modify focus and exposure, you must do it effectively to Focus on the most crucial components of the complete picture.

The task is that every photograph takes a specific method of focus and exposure setting. Things that work notably for landscapes don't work almost as properly for night or tour photos.

How to Lock Focus and Exposure with AE/AF Lock

The iPhone also allows you to lock each one of the appealing points; focus and exposure. So why would you need to close those functions while going for a picture?

- The principle motive is if anything changes in the scene, including a moving subject or altered lighting, your focus and exposure would stay unchanged.

- That's why it's a great idea to lock Focus and exposure when you're expecting motion within the picture. For instance, *Focus and exposure* lock could be beneficial in street picture taking.

- You might frame the shot, and set the focus and exposure earlier, then obviously watch out for a person to pass-by before taking your photo.

- Once you've locked the focus and exposure, you might take several pictures of the same image and never have to set focus and exposure each time you want to consider photos. To unlock Focus and exposure, select anywhere on the screen.

- To lock focus and exposure, Tap and retain your hands on the display screen for mere multiple seconds at the stage where you want to create the centre point. A yellowish package with AE/AF lock can look near the top of the display.

Note: You can nevertheless swipe up or down on display to regulate exposure manually.

*Now regardless of what happens within the framework or how you fling the iPhone 8, iPhone 8 Pro, and iPhone 8 Pro Max, the **Focus and Exposure** would still be unchanged.*

How to Take HDR Photos

HDR, which means ***High Active Range**,* is another incredible picture tool that is included in the camera of your iPhone.

HDR picture taking with the iPhone combines three unique exposures of precisely the same image to produce one nicely exposed picture.

It's exquisite for high comparison moments with shiny and darkish areas since it allows you to capture extra components in both shadows and the highlights fully.

Some small adjustments within an editing application such as Snapseed can indeed draw out the colours and detail that were captured in the **HDR photograph**, although it still comes with fantastic well-balanced exposure.

- You'll find the HDR setting on the left side of the camera app. Tapping on HDR provides you with three options: Motion, ON, or OFF.

- Notably, it's high-quality to use HDR for panorama or landscape pictures and scenes where the sky occupies a significant area of the photograph. This enables the taking of extra fine detail in both the brighter sky and the darker foreground.

- There are a few downsides to HDR, especially in

conditions of pictures of motion. Because HDR is a variety of three sequentially captured photos, you might encounter "ghosts" if the picture is changing quickly. HDR images also require a long period to capture, which means that your hands may shake even while the shutter is open up.

- It's additionally essential to state that non-HDR pictures will sometimes look much better than HDR ones, that's the reason it's a good idea to save lots of each variation of the image. To make sure that each variant is stored, go to configurations > photos & camera, and ensure Save Normal Picture is **ON** in the *HDR section*.

- It's also well worth mentioning that the default iPhone camera application comes with an alternatively subtle *HDR impact,* a sophisticated camera application that can create much more powerful HDR results and provide you with complete control over the catch.

How to Take Snapshot in Burst Mode

- Burst mode is one of the very most useful capturing features in the iPhone camera app. It enables you to take ten images in only one second, which makes it easy to capture the suitable movement shot with reduced blur entirely.

- If you wish to activate a *burst setting*, press down the shutter button for half a second or longer, and the iPhone begins capturing one after another. When you've shot a burst of snap photos, after that, you can choose the lovely images from the Set and delete others.

- Burst setting is worth using each time there's any

movement or unpredictability in the picture.

Remember utilizing it when photographing kids, animals, birds, and splashing water.

It's also excellent for taking pictures on magical occasions in street picture taking. Likewise, try the utilization of burst setting to capture the correct stride or present.

How to Take Pictures with Volume Buttons

Perhaps you have ever overlooked or missed the iPhone's tiny on-display shutter button? If so, change to the utilization of volume control keys beside your iPhone.

Either of these buttons can be utilized for shutter release, and the tactile opinions you get from pressing this button is a great deal more pleasurable than pressing an electronic switch.

Additionally, this enables you to carry the iPhone with two hands, just as you'd grab a typical digital camera.

The only drawback of the approach is that you'll require pressing the Volume button pretty hard, which might produce camera shake. That's especially essential in a low-mild or less lighted environment, where any movement of your iPhone would lead to the blurry picture.

How to take Photographs with your Apple Headphones

Remember those white apple headphones that were included with your iPhone, on purchase can be utilized for photo taking. It additionally has *Volume buttons*, and you may use these control keys to consider photos!

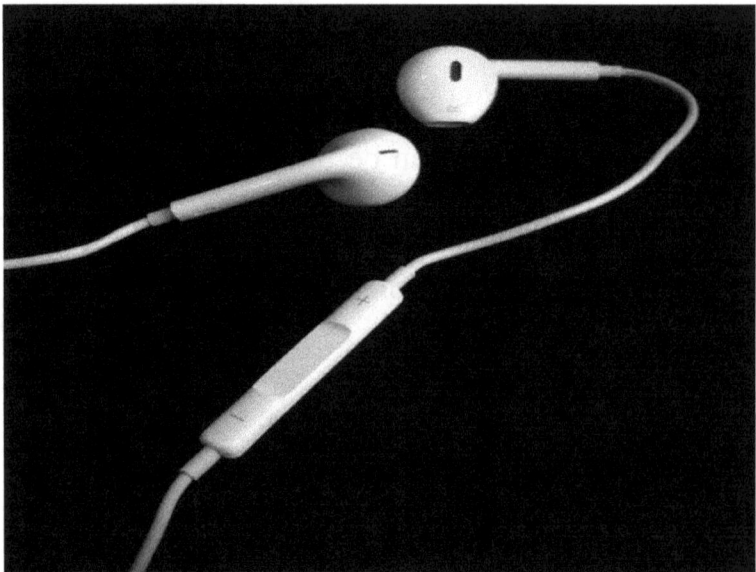

This feature is tremendously useful when you need to take discreet pictures of people you don't recognize or know in person, as you could pretend to be paying focused attention to music or making a call while you're taking pictures.

This method additionally is available when your iPhone is on a tripod. As you release the shutter with your headphones, you can get rid of any unintentional digital camera movement, which is quite essential for night time pictures, long exposure images, etc.

CHAPTER 15

How to Use iPhone Portrait Mode to Make Blurry Background

The **iPhone portrait mode** is the correct device to make brilliant looking portrait photographs with your iPhone. The portrait setting allows you to produce a shallow depth of field in your pictures quickly. This leads to an excellent blurry background that could typically be performed with a **DSLR camera**. With this section, you'll see how to use the iPhone portrait setting to make a professional-looking iPhone photo with a beautiful background blur.

What's Portrait Mode?

Portrait mode is a distinctive capturing mode available in the native camera application of an iPhone. It creates the use of a unique **Depth Impact Tool** to make a shallow Depth of field in your pictures.

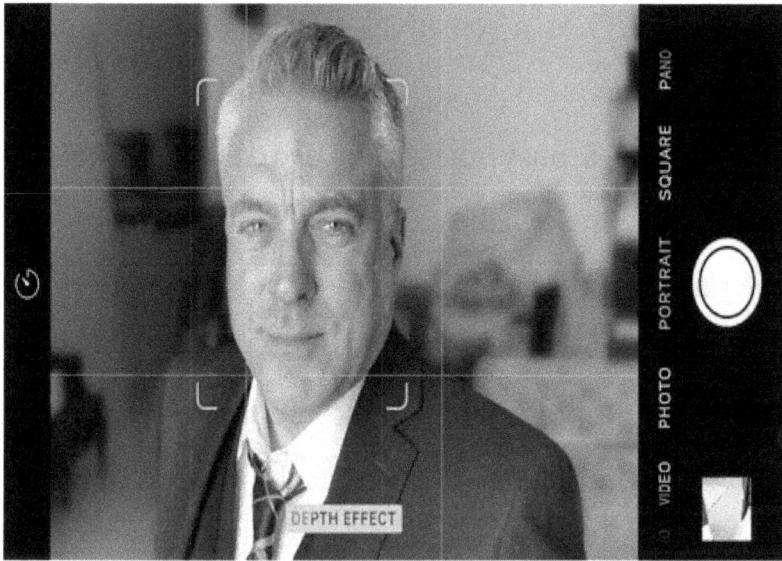

Shallow depth of field means that only a little area of the photo is within focus as the other is blurred. More often than not, you'll need your most significant concern at the mercy of appearing in razor-sharp focus as the background shows up blurred.

This soft and tender blurry background is categorized as **"bokeh,"** which originates from the Japanese language.

Why Should You Use Shallow Depth of Field?

Portrait photographers often utilize the **shallow depth of field**. Why? Since it places the focus on the average person and creates a sensitive, dreamy background in it. Blurring the context is also truly useful when taking in locations with a busy, messy, or distracting background. The blurring makes the context secondary, getting the viewer's attention back to the main subject matter in the foreground.

Shallow Depth of Field isn't something you'd use for every kind of picture. You typically wouldn't want a blurry Background in scenery or architectural photo as you'd want to see everything vividly from foreground to Background.

However, in portrait pictures, a Shallow Depth of Field can make a significant distinction to the result of your photo. By blurring the background, you may make your subject matter stand out.

How to Make Background Blur on iPhone

Sometimes back, the iPhone camera hasn't allowed you to have any control over the depth of field for your pictures. You've had the choice to have everything in Focus - unless your most significant subject matter comes very near the zoom lens; in such case, the background seems blurred.

However, with portrait setting on the new iPhone, now you can pick and choose what's in focus and what isn't. This gives you unprecedented control over your iPhone, permitting you to mimic the appearance of DSLR cameras that can catch a shallow depth of field.

While portrait mode is most beneficial when planning on taking pictures of humans, pets, nature, etc., it can be utilized to blur the background behind any subject.

Many things appear better when there's a soft, dreamy background in it - especially if that background could distract the viewer from the primary subject.

How to use iPhone Portrait Mode

- Developing a shallow **Depth of Field** with Portrait mode on the iPhone is super easy. You can start by starting the default camera app, then swipe through the taking pictures modes (video, picture, etc.) until Portrait is highlighted in yellow.

- The very first thing you'll notice when you switch

to Portrait Setting is that everything gets enlarged. That's because the camera automatically switches to the iPhone's 2x Telephoto Zoom lens. The telephoto zoom lens typically creates more flattering portrait images than the huge-angle zoom lens that could distort cosmetic features.

- You'll additionally spot the words **Depth Impact** appears at the bottom of the screen. Moreover, your telephone will help you give on-screen instructions in case you don't have things framed up optimally for an enjoyable portrait shot. For instance, you'll possibly see Move Farther Away or even more Light Required:

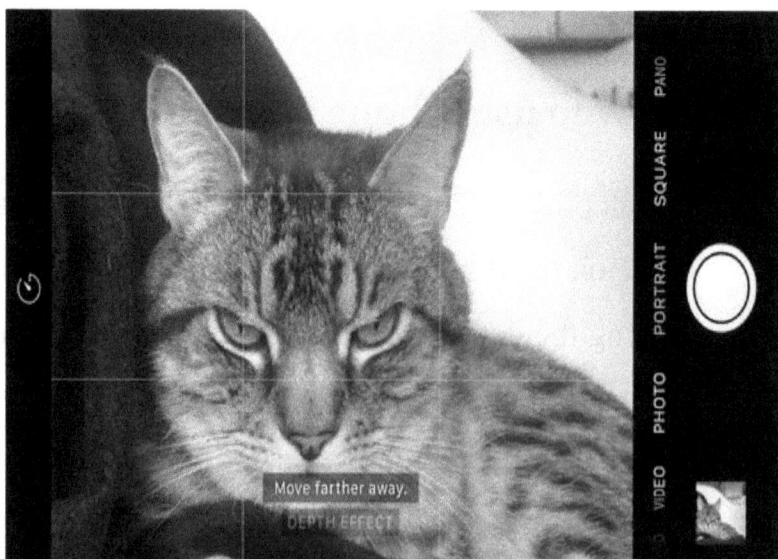

- The moment you're at the right distance from your subject, the words **Depth Effect** would be highlighted in yellow. You'll also see four yellow crop marks, indicating the face of your subject:

- You're now ready to take, so select the shutter button to consider your picture. After making the picture, you'll observe that two variations of the image can look in the camera app. One image will have the *Depth Impact* (blurred Background), and the other won't.

- Evaluating those two versions of the image

sincerely suggests how nice a portrait picture shows up when it has a **Shallow Depth of Field**.

- If for reasons unknown you're not sure which of both pictures had the **Depth impact**, it'll be labelled in your image Set as shown below:

Tips For Creating Background Blur

When taking photos with the iPhone portrait mode, it's essential to think about your background plus your subject. The type of Background you choose against its distance from your subject matter, will each have a significant effect on the final image.

The **Depth Effect** in Portrait mode is most effective when your subject matter is not the background. The further away the topic is from the background, the more delightful blur you'll get. Spot the difference in the background blur of the two pictures:

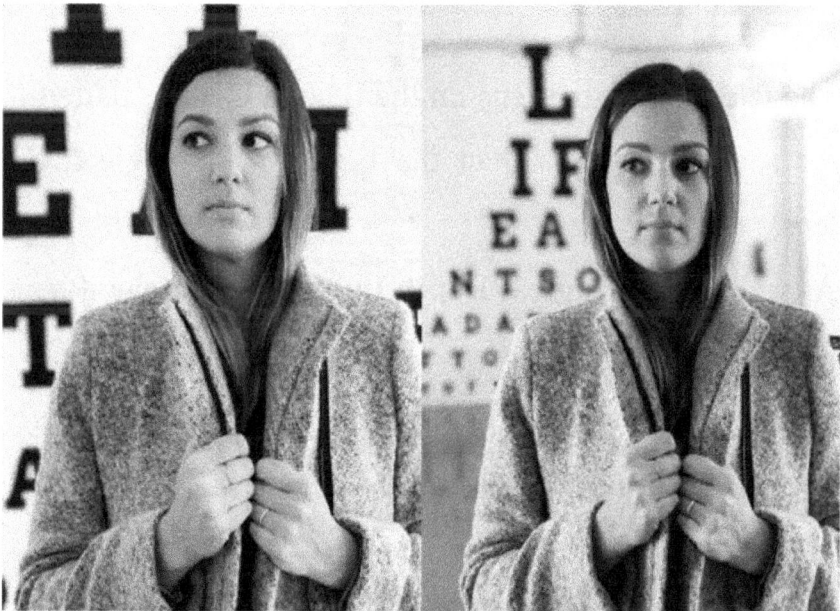

Subject close to background   Subject farther away from background

So; if your Background doesn't show up blurry enough when taking photos in a portrait setting, move your subject matter further from the background.

It's additionally essential to have something in the background so that there are a few components for the camera to blur.

Conclusively; the iPhone has continuously been a first-rate device for most types of picture taking - such as landscape, structures, and street picture taking. However, now the iPhone provides the potential to take amazing, high-quality portrait photos.

The telephoto zoom lens on the iPhone is more flattering for shooting people than the typical wide-angle zoom lens.

As well as the **Magical Depth Impact tool** on the iPhone Portrait Mode creates a lovely background blur - simulating the shallow depth of field that could formerly only be performed with a DSLR camera.

Taking photos with the iPhone portrait mode is a delight.

Moreover, your subject will be thrilled when you suggest to them how beautiful they show up in your photos.

Don't forget; even while Portrait mode is the perfect setting when planning on taking pictures of individuals, pets, nature, etc., you can use it on any subject matter in which you require to make an attractive *background blur*.

CHAPTER 16

How to Shoot Unique iPhone Photos

Hipstamatic is an elegant iPhone camera application for growing unique photos with a retro or vintage appearance. It comes with an outstanding selection of analogue film, zoom lens, and flash results, which enable you to easily change an ordinary picture into something exceedingly thrilling, stunning or dramatic. Besides, it comes with an accessible improving and editing Set for fine-tuning your photographs in post-processing. With this section, you'll learn the step-by-step instructions when planning on taking pictures and editing and enhancing lovely images using the Hipstamatic app.

Hipstamatic Zoom Lens & Film Combos

Hipstamatic is most beneficially known because of its potential to make a vast selection of retro-styled pictures based on numerous filters. The filter systems are applied when you take the photo; nevertheless, you can always change the ultimate result by just selecting different filter systems once you've used the shot.

The Hipstamatic filters get into three categories that are: zoom lens type, film type, and flash type. Before you proceed with going for a picture in Hipstamatic, you should select which zoom lens, film, and flash you want to use.

The lens decides the colours and tones in your photo. The film determines the framework or vignette across the advantage of the image (and occasionally also changes the colours of the image). The flash helps in creating distinctive lights.

The lens, film, and flash mixtures in Hipstamatic are known as "*combos.*" Through the utilization of diverse combinations of the zoom lens, film, and flash, you can create an enormous variety of image styles - from faded superior results to high comparison dark and white pictures.

To give an example of how Hipstamatic can change an ordinary picture into something a lot more aesthetically attractive, check the photographs below. The first picture is the original photo without Hipstamatic filter systems applied:

Subsequent are a few examples of the same scene captured with the use of specific Hipstamatic lens and film combos:

When taking a picture with Hipstamatic, you can either permit the app to select a combo for you or try different mixtures of your desire until you locate an impact you like.

Hipstamatic includes a core set of lenses, film and flash options, and many more can be found as in-app purchases.

Selecting A Camera Interface

Hipstamatic has two different camera settings/interfaces included in the application. You may use the vintage camera user interface that mimics the appearance and feel of old film cameras:

You can likewise Utilize the *Pro camera interface,* which has a modern and professional feel. This camera mode is excellent if you want a bit of manual control while taking pictures:

If you wish to select from both camera settings, Tap both opposing arrows icon (arrows are either facing each other or aside depending on which digital camera setting you are employing).

How to Take Pictures with Hipstamatic Vintage Camera

You are going to learn how to consider pictures using the vintage camera mode in Hipstamatic. Be sure you've chosen the primary camera interface. If you're presently in the pro camera setting, select the opposing arrows to change to a traditional setting.

When working with Classic mode, you can change between your front and back views of the camera by Tapping the flip icon (curved arrow) in the bottom right of the screen.

How to Take a Picture with Basic Camera

- When you point the camera at a picture, you'll view it in the *sq. Viewfinder*. When capturing, you can choose from viewfinder alternatives.

- You can both view the picture with no filter

systems (lenses, movies, etc.) applied, alternatively, you can see in real-time, what the actual photograph can look like following when the shot has been taken using your chosen filters (you'll understand how to select lens, movies, etc. later as you read further).

- To change between those two viewfinder options, Tap the small dark switch in the bottom right of the viewfinder (as shown below):

When the switch is at the **OFF** function (completely black colour), you won't start to see the picture with all of your selected filters applied, but, when the photograph is used, the filters will be employed to the image when the switch is within the ON position (yellow eyeball icon will be shown).

I endorse getting the viewfinder change in the ON position, and that means you can easily see the impact of the existing zoom lens, film, and flash combo.

When you've composed your shot, take the picture by Tapping the yellow shutter button at the very top right.

NB: You can additionally enlarge the viewfinder by double-Tapping the viewfinder windows. You'll be able to select the viewer once to consider the shot.

If you wish to start to see the picture you've taken, Tap the square image thumbnail icon in the bottom still left of the screen. The image gallery can look displaying a preview of the photos you've shot with Hipstamatic, as shown below.

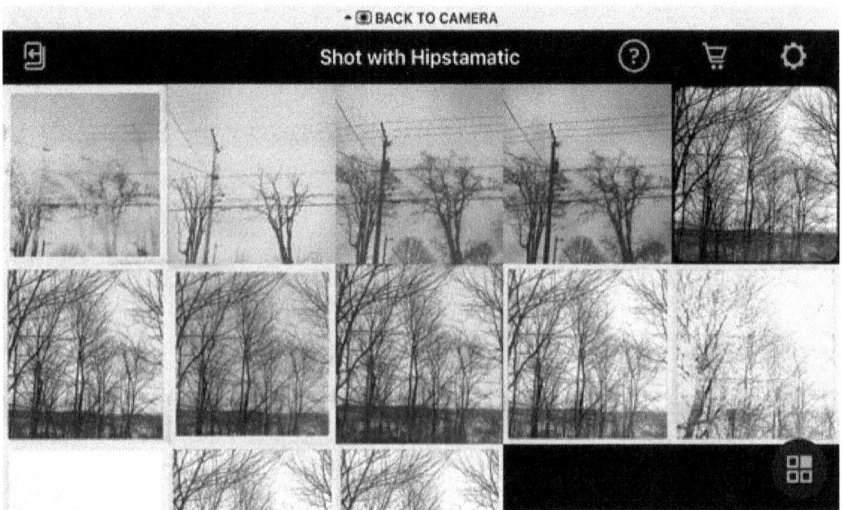

If you wish to see a much larger model of a specific photo, select the picture you want to see.

When viewing the entire sized image, you'll see which film/zoom lens/flash combo used, as well as the location where the picture was taken.

How to Decide on a Zoom lens/Film/Flash Combo

- For you to specify the appearance and design of your picture, you'll need to pick from the several options of lens and film (and flash if preferred).

- You can either decide on a preset combo from the favorites screen, or you create your combo from scrape. Taking into consideration the preset combo, first of all, begin by Tapping the circular icon (the next from the cheapest right-hand part) as shown in the red group below:

- Swipe across to see the number of cameras with diverse zoom lens/film/flash combos, however; don't Tap on the cameras yet. Every camera comes with an example photo showing the type of picture style that unique combo will generate.

- Tap and keep a camera to see more information in what configurations to be Utilized, then select the x to come back to the standard display screen.

- To select a specific combo from the favorites screen, Tap on the camera combo you want to use. On the other hand, you can allow the app to shuffle the combo on every occasion arbitrarily you are taking picture shot, providing you with a definite effect for every chance. If you like this option, select the shuffle icon (two arrows at the top right) and pick your chosen option:

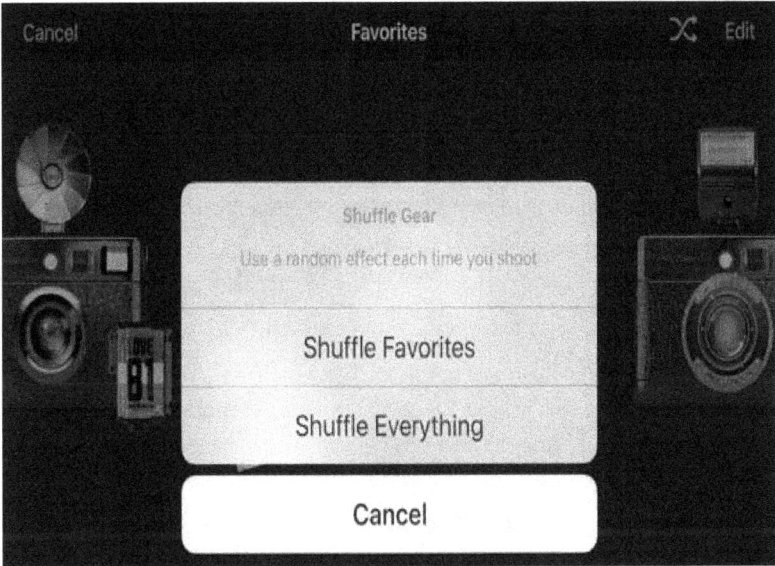

- When you've chosen a camera combo from the listed favorites, or the shuffle option, you'll be taken back to the camera to be able to begin capturing.

- You can additionally create your own lens/film/flash combos and upload these to the report on favorites. To achieve that, Tap the spherical icon (second from right hands side) at the bottom of the screen to access the preferences display.

- Swipe over the cameras to the much right, then select the newest favorites (+) icon.

- The proceeding screen will show a preview image with three icons beneath it. From still left to right, these icons are **Zoom lens, Film, Flash.**

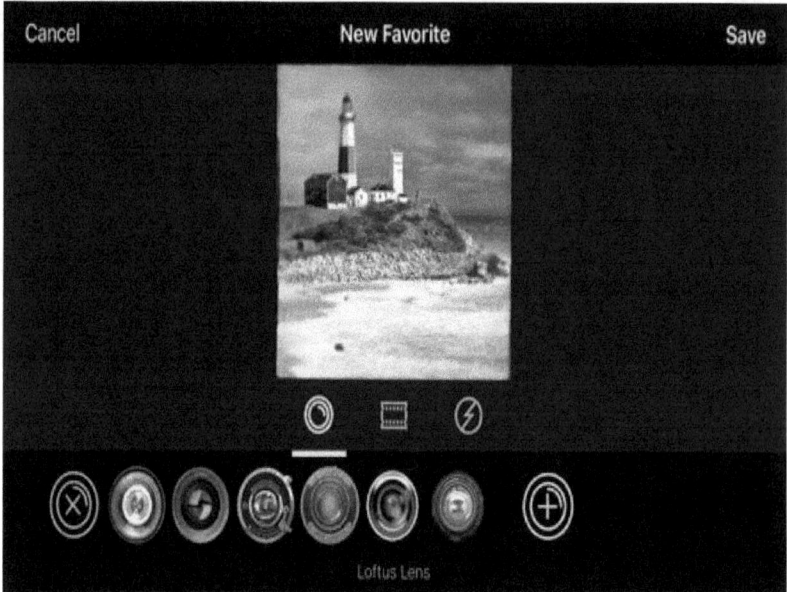

- Begin by selecting the type of zoom lens that you want to use - recollect that the zoom lens adjusts the colors and shades of your picture when you choose the particular lens at the bottom of the screen, the preview image changes showing what impact that zoom lens could have on your photo.

- When you've chosen the lens that you like, Tap the Film icon (middle icon) under the picture preview. The film determines the framework or vignette round the advantage of the image, and additionally, it may change the firmness. Pick the film style that you want from underneath of the display:

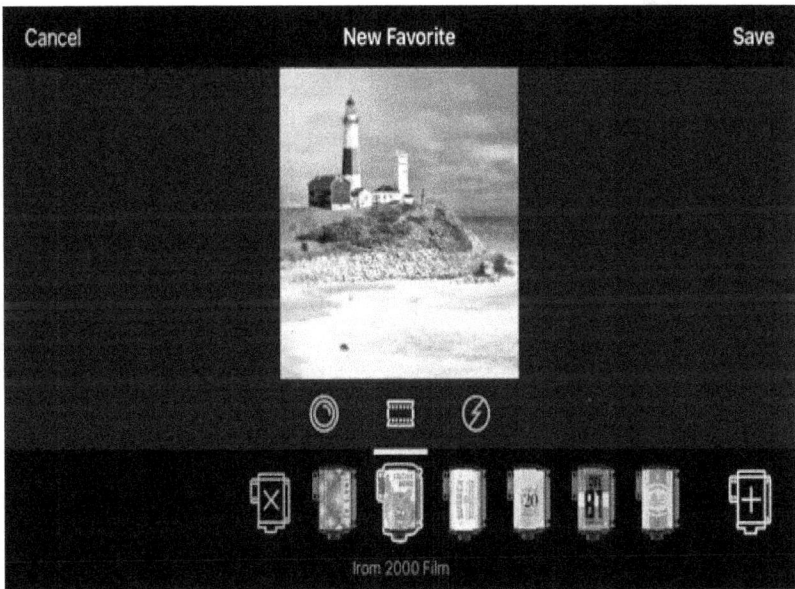

- Next, select the flash icon (right-hand icon) under the image preview. The flashes put in a particular lightning impact on your picture. If you wish to apply flash, choose your decision from underneath of the display, typically, select No Flash.

- You'll discover that there's an advantage (+) indication for the zoom lens, film and flash options - Tapping this icon goes to the Hipstamatic store where you can buy new lenses, movies, and flashes to increase your Sets.

- When you're pleased with your selected combo, Tap Save at the very top right part of the screen. On the next screen, you can enter a name for your combo, then select Done:

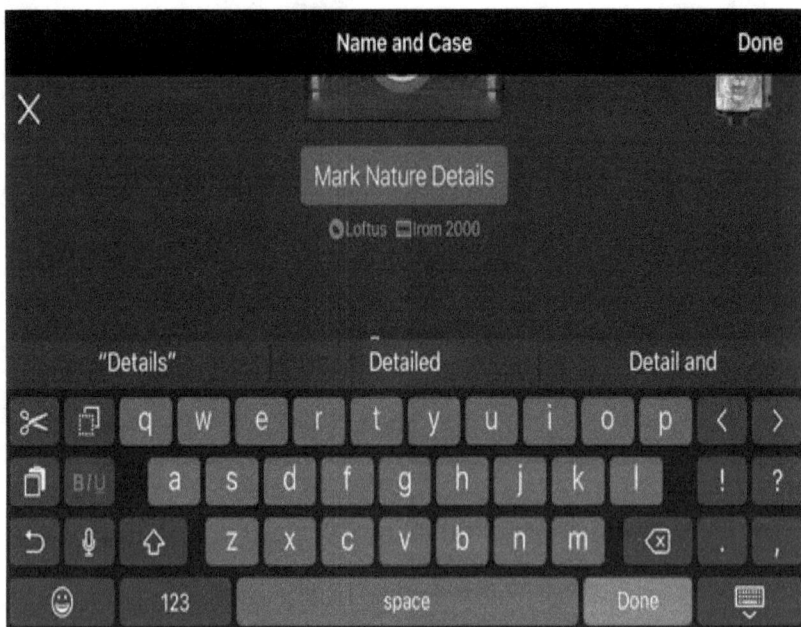

- Your newly added combo can look in the set of Favourites. To use this combo, select onto it, and also you'll be taken back to the camera and that means you can begin snapping:

- There's one other method of choosing a combo of a zoom lens, film and flash for capturing. Remember, there's a back view and front side view in traditional camera setting - on the back camera view, Tap the **Turn icon** (curved arrow in the bottom right) that may change you to the leading camera view.

- To select a particular zoom lens, swipe over the large zoom lens in the center of the display till you start to see the zoom lens you desire.

- To choose a film, select the film icon at the still left of the display screen. Swipe up or down on the rolls of the film until you find the lens you wish.

- To find out more records regarding a specific film, as well as test pictures, Tap the motion of the film - select Done to exit the film information.

- When you've selected the film you want to use, Tap the camera body at the right of the screen to return to the leading camera view.

- To select away a flash, select the **Flash icon** (second from lower still left) then swipe over the distinctive flash options. If you don't want to use flash, choose the No Flash option. Tap Done to come back to the leading camera view.

- If you wish to buy more lenses, movies, and flashes to increase your Sets, Tap the **SHOPPING CART SOFTWARE** icon (second from bottom level right). You will see the presented products or click on a particular item if you wish to exit the shopping cart software, Tap **Done**.

- When you're content with the zoom lens/film/flash combo which you've selected, select the **Flip icon** (curved arrow in the bottom right) to come back to the back camera view, then start taking pictures!

How to Switch Flash ON & OFF

When you're capturing with the back camera view, you'll observe a black colour slider below the sq. Viewfinder. This will help you to select if the flash should be brought ON or not if you are going for a picture.

Whenever the flash slider reaches the center, the flash is powered down.

When the flash slider is moved left, your selected flash

effect will be applied to the photo; however, the flash at the front end of your iPhone X Series won't fire on.

When the flash slider is moved to the right, your selected flash effect will be employed to the photograph, and the flash at the front end of your iPhone X Series will fire to provide more light on your subject.

How to Change Shutter Speed

- At the very top right of the camera, the display is the **shutter speed dial**. Modifying the shutter rate does a couple of things - it changes the exposure of the image (how gleaming it seems) and impacts how motion is captured.

- The lower the Volume on the dial, the slower the shutter speed. A slow shutter acceleration results in a brighter image, and an effortless shutter swiftness leads into a darker picture. You might use this feature to produce artistically shiny photos or very darkish moody pictures.

- Inside a case where you're capturing a scene with moving subjects, a natural shutter rate will freeze movement, and a sluggish shutter rate will capture the action as a blur.

How to Create Multiple Exposures

Hipstamatic gives you to generate thrilling dual exposure pictures. You take two different pictures, and then your camera combines them. That is a fun strategy to apply and can result in some exciting artwork and abstract images.

- To begin with, creating this kind of photograph, slide the **Multiple Exposure switch** (at the top left-hand side of the camera display) left such that it turns yellowish:

- Take your first picture by Tapping the yellow shutter button at the right. You will notice that the multiple exposure switch has moved to the right such that only half of the yellow square is seen:

- Position your camera at a different subject matter or view, then take the next shot. You'll start to see the "**Multi Revealing**" message show up as the app combines both images.

- If you wish to view the two times exposure image on your gallery, select the square model thumbnail icon at the bottom left of the screen. Tap the yellow pub near the top of the gallery to come back to the camera.

- Given that you're familiar with the functions of the vintage camera user interface, let's consider the procedure of taking pictures with the *Pro camera mode.*

How to Take Pictures with Hipstamatic Pro Camera

Hipstamatic pro camera mode gives more advanced camera application that gives you more manual control when shooting pictures.

- If you're presently using the Vintage camera mode, change to the pro camera user interface by just Tapping both opposing arrows at the low area of the screen as shown below:

- The pro digital camera interface appears very distinctive to the classic interface which doesn't have any retro styling, but has a larger square viewfinder with icons around the edges:

- Let's begin the usage of those camera icons to customize the final picture. In case you're using the camera in landscape orientation, as shown above, the top-right icon allows you to change the **Aspect Ratio**:

- The Aspect ratio decides the width and height of images. Choosing the 1:1 aspect percentage will result in an excellent square image, as the 16:9 proportion will be full than its elevation. The next icon in the red circle below gives you to choose different flash options, including *Flash On, Flash Auto,* and *Constant Light*:

The icon under the flash icon will help you to switch to the front camera to be able to have a self-portrait. While in the bottom right of the display will be the two opposing arrows that may take you back to the **Classic vintage style** camera.

The icon in the bottom left of the screen gives you to choose which zoom lens/film/flash combo you should employ - similar from what you did with the entire classic camera mode:

After Tapping the icon, you can progressively swipe

through the various combos until you locate an effect that suits your interest, or Tap the plus (+) icon to create a new combo. Tap on the combo you want to apply to return to the camera:

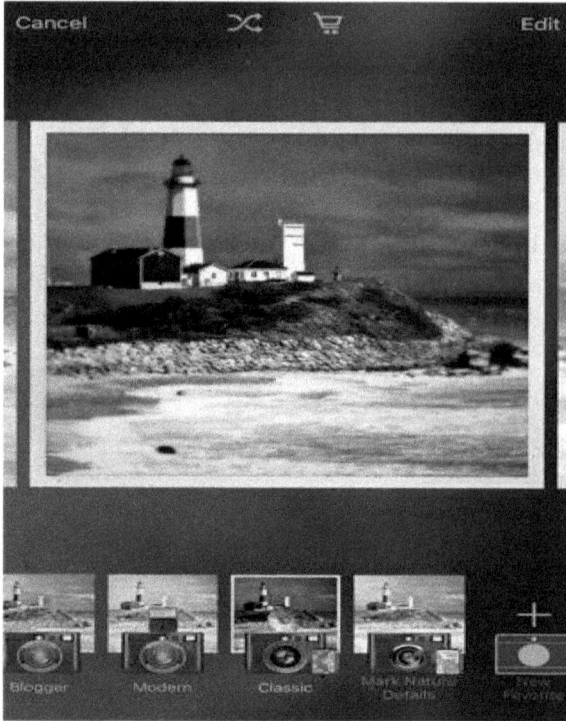

The **"M"** icon (at the right-hand side of the shutter button as shown below) stands for **Manual**, and it permits you to fine-tune the camera settings before taking your shot:

When you Tap the **Manual (m)** icon, a bar of icons will appear in its place:

The **round target icon** allows you to adjust the focus manually. The **magnifying glass icon** helps you to zoom in. Each of these settings is modified by making use of the slider at the bottom of the display screen.

The **+/- icon** turns on the exposure slider which lets you alter the brightness up or down for brighter or darker photographs:

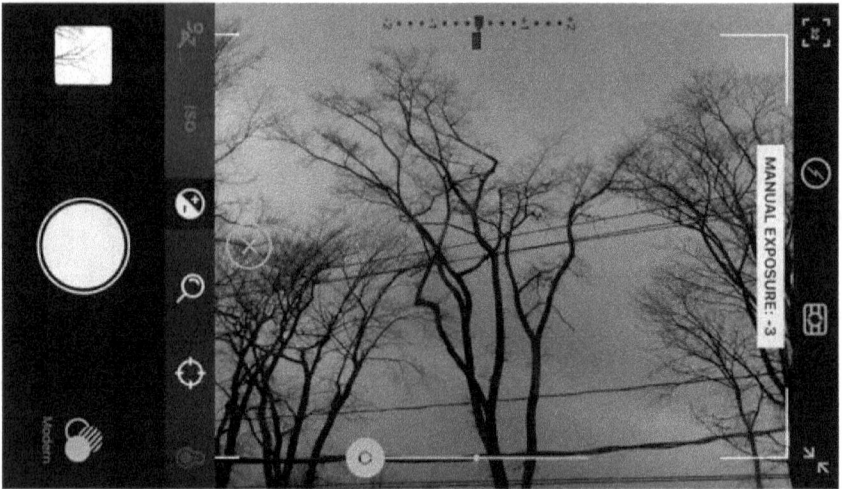

For the fun part! The **ISO** and **Shutter Speed** (running man icon) settings allow you to manage and control exposure and how motion appears in your photograph:

- If you wish to create motion blur when photographing an instant running subject matter, you'll need a *slow shutter speed* and a *minimal ISO* (a minimum ISO facilitates preventing the picture from being over-exposed).

- To begin with, select the **ISO icon**, and use the slider to lessen the ISO to the lowest selection of number feasible. Then Tap the Shutter Rate icon (operating man) and move the slider to reduce the shutter rate to ensure that the picture appears almost too bright.

- The reason behind this is that; the brighter the picture, the slower the shutter acceleration, which equals higher movement blur of moving topics.

- If you're capturing in fantastic daytime conditions, you will learn that your sluggish shutter images appear too vibrant. That is why it's typically more comfortable to take at dawn or nightfall, or on darkish overcast times, to fully capture excellent show shutter photos.

- The final camera function is White Balance (lamp icon) that allows you to change the shade temperature on the scale from blue to yellow:

- The white balance enables you to warm up or keep down the colors, either to get perfect color balance or for creative impact. You can pull the slider left to help make the colors warmer (i.e., more yellow), and move to the right to make sure they are more refreshing (i.e., extra blue):

This is undoubtedly a proper setting for indoor capturing situations where the scene is illuminated by using artificial light with a yellow coloration cast. You can merely pull the white balance slider till you're pleased with the color firmness shown in the viewfinder:

How to Edit Pictures in Hipstamatic

Hipstamatic isn't taken into account as a professionally graded picture editor. It merely has a significant number of user-friendly improving features that will help you get the images simply perfect, such as the potential to choose a different combo such as zoom lens, film, and flash you can use when planning on taking pictures.

- To access the modifying mode, whether or not you're using the vintage camera or the pro camera, select the sq. Image thumbnail, which ultimately shows the previous picture taken:

- In the image gallery, Tap the picture you need to edit, then Tap the edit icon (3 circles) at the lowest part of the display screen as shown below:

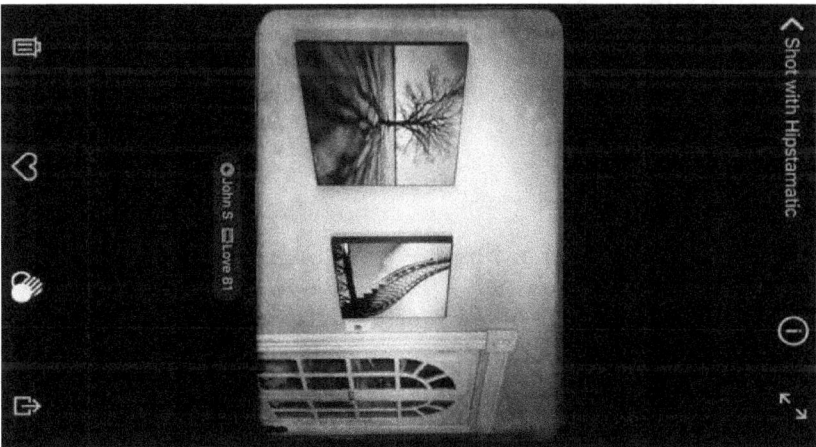

- Swipe through the preset combos at the bottom of the screen, Tapping on any that you prefer to see what impact it is wearing your image. Once you've chosen a preset that you want, use the slider to change the strength of the result till you're content with the final result. Tap **Save** when you're done editing.

- Much like the one-Tap presets, there are a few other modifying alternatives that you can use to improve your picture. Tap the edit icon (three circles), then select the choice icon (three sliders) situated merely above the configurations icon.
- Below your image, you'll visit a row of icons that may be used to fine-tune and edit the photo.
- Conclusively, Hipstamatic gives you to create an array of picture patterns, which include retro, classic, and dark and white.
- The application has two different kinds of camera settings (classic and pro), to be able to select to shoot using whichever interface you like. Each parameter can help you choose a zoom lens/film/flash combo, to enable you always to create the complete appearance and feel that you envisioned.
- The editing tools in the application enable you to

fine-tune the picture when you've taken the shot, with the choice to decorate and improve the effect you used - or completely change the totality of the picture. With such a great deal of unique visual combos presented within this app, you can create excellent images, indeed with an incredible artistic edge.

CHAPTER 17

How to Use Superimpose Apps for Blending Images on iPhone

The superimpose application offers a fantastic group of gear for combining two iPhone photographs into a variety of approaches. You might change the background around your subject matter, put in a creative consistency overlay, or create a distinctive double exposure that mixes two photographs collectively. Superimpose additionally provides fundamental editing alternatives, including preset filters and color and exposure adjustments. With this section, you'll locate a way to use the superimpose application to replace the background in your iPhone photos and create an incredible double exposure impact.

How to Replace the Background of an Image

You can replace the background in virtually any iPhone picture with this process you are going to learn, which works satisfactorily with photos which have a smooth structure and a solid colour contrast between your subject and the background.

Follow the step-by-step instructions below meticulously.

Import Your Photos

When you open the superimpose app, you'll note there are four predominant areas as shown below that are *Home, Transform, Mask, and Filtering*. The application begins inside the home section, and that means you can import your pictures:

- When working on a superimposes app, you will need to open both a background and a foreground picture. For the substance of changing background, the background image is the picture that will become the newest background. The foreground picture is the picture with most of your subject.

- To import your snap photos, ensure you're within the home portion of superimposing, then select the import icon (can be found at the top level of the screen). A section entitled import background can look close to the very best of the screen:

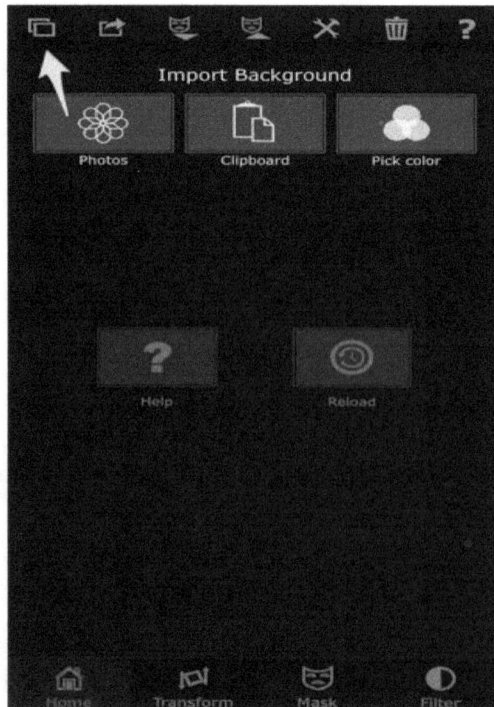

- In the import background section, Tap images to access your iPhone's picture library, then choose the photo you need to use as your background picture.

- When you insert or attach the background picture, you'll see its dimensions. If you wish to exchange the dimensional level, select Constraints for growth of varied size choice or crop the image as you want. In case your background-size doesn't require any modification, Tap **Choose**:

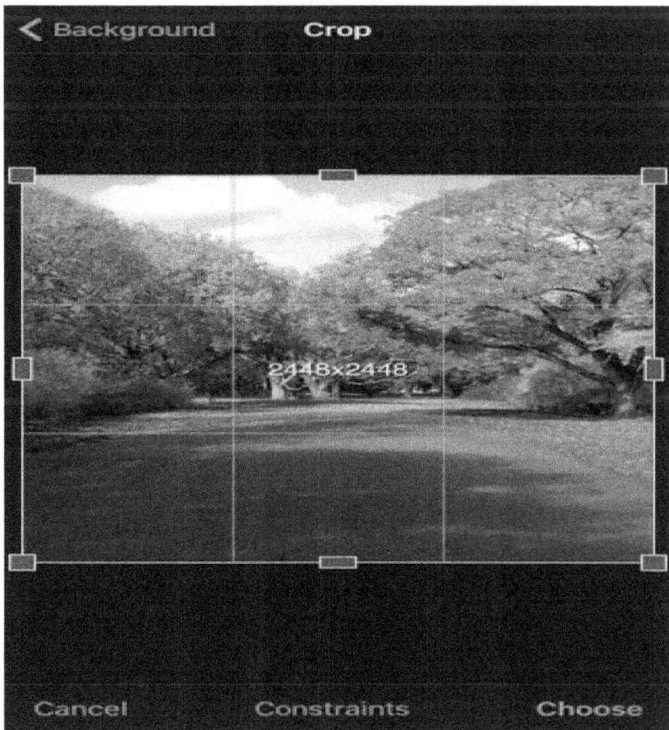

- Subsequently, you will have to import your foreground photograph. Tap the import icon again (it's located at the left of the display) and also you'll see a segment titled **import foreground** near the top of the display:

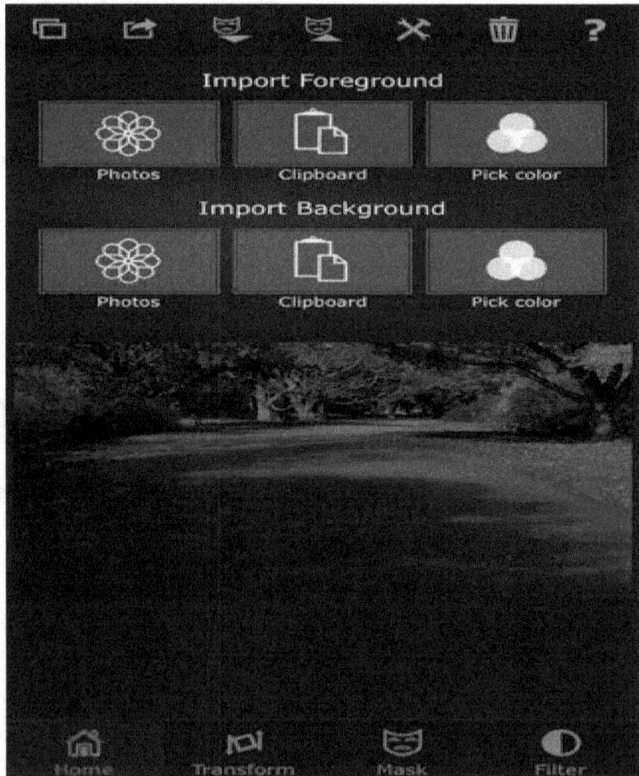

- Within the import foreground phase, Tap **Pictures**, then pick the image you wish to apply as your foreground photo.

Once more, you can crop the picture, resize it by using the **Constraints** choice, or Tap **Choose**:

Now, you'll see that your foreground picture is superimposed over the background image:

How to Reposition Foreground Image

Now you can resize and reposition the foreground image, and that means you can have it in the right position over the background image. For you to now access the resizing and repositioning tools, select the Transform option at the bottom of the screen.

You'll remember that the foreground picture will have deals on the edges (for resizing) and the sides (for rotating). If you wish to move the foreground image around, pull the image with your finger. The image may also be resized by pinching in and from the picture.

Near the top of the Transform display, you'll observe seven different icons. These are:

- **Undo**: This function is to undo your last action.
- **Redo:** This function is to redo your previous action.
- **Merge:** This function is to merge the background and foreground photos collectively with the reason to weigh another foreground picture at the very top. That's useful if you want to add extra layers to your image.
- **Swap:** This functions carefully turn the foreground picture horizontally or vertically, besides, to change the background and foreground photos.
- **Place at the Middle:** This function will position the foreground image within the guts of the background photo.
- **Fit to Background:** This function will level the foreground picture to the same size as the

background.

- **Configurations:** This function will change the transparency and blend setting, which would be needed for developing dual exposure images.

How to Produce Masks

The masking feature will enable you to edit and control the transparency of different sections of the foreground image(s).

When you make an integral part of the foreground picture transparent, the background image below will be seen. Quite merely, masking provides you with the liberty to remove undesirable servings of the foreground images.

You can perform this by Tapping the Mask option at the lowest area of the screen, then subsequently Tap the *Magic Wand icon* close to the right hand, which is below it to get access to the masking tools:

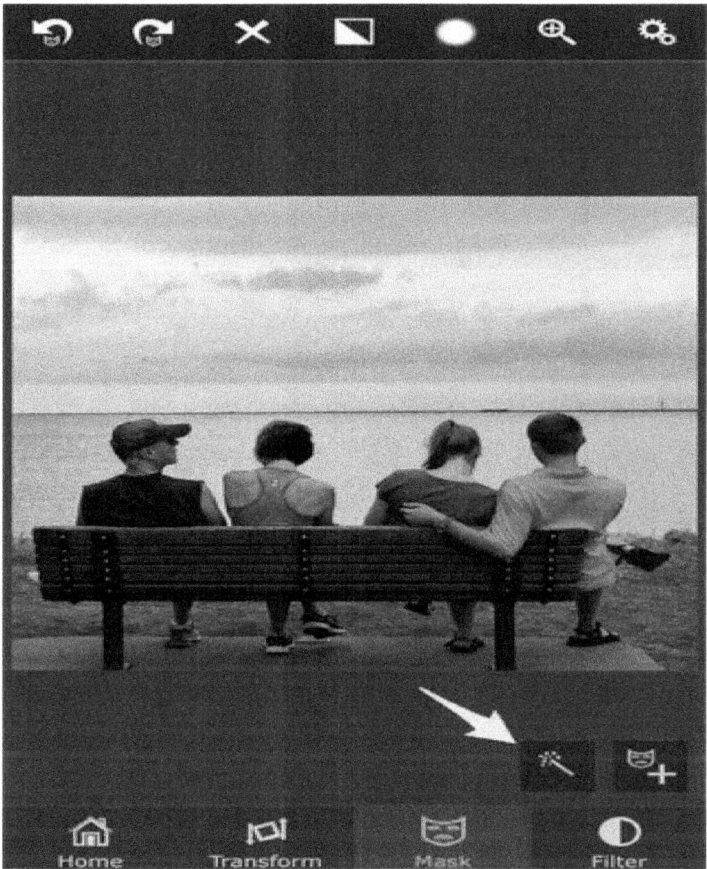

NB: There are six simple masking tools which are accessible (the top six tools are displayed in the pop-up menu, as shown below):

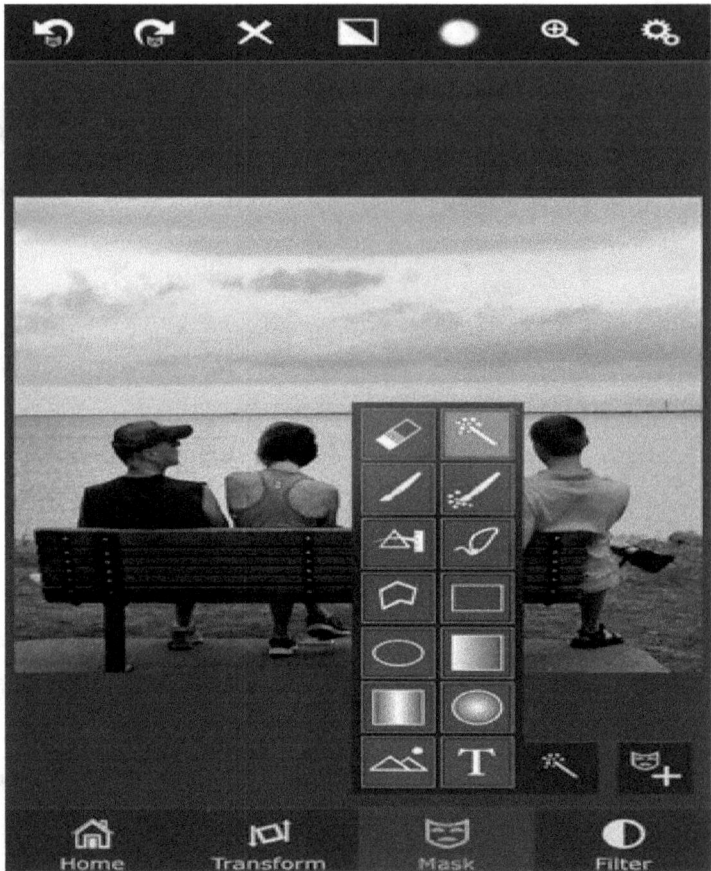

Below is a brief explanation of the six masking tools:

- **Eraser:** This tool will erase any errors you've manufactured in masking.

- **Magic Wand:** This function will mask all the similar coloration pixels encircling any point you Tap. You can drag or select to use the tool.

- **Brush:** Covers the whole area much, just like a brush. This tool doesn't recognize sides, so it's much useful for masking more significant regions.

- **Smart Brush:** This feature is comparable to the brush tool, but it recognizes the sides of the areas you're masking. Its function is to permit your selected exact locations and minimizes unintended or **unintentional brush strokes.**

- **Colour Range:** This function is similar to the magic wand tool, but instead of just the encompassing pixels, it selects all pixels related to the picture that fits the colour of the pixel you Tap.

- **Lasso:** This feature will help you to pull a freehand lasso and mask anything in or from the lasso loop.

NB: Every one of the tools has configurations ascribed to it. When you've chosen the masking tool, you want to use, Tap the configurations icon (can be found at the top right corner of the screen). The configurations for the tool can be seen close to underneath the screen, as shown below:

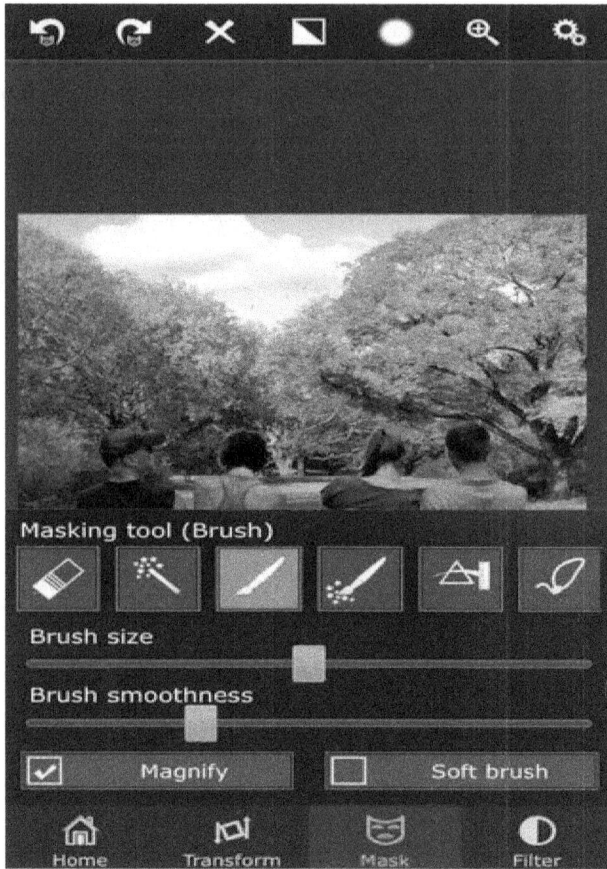

For example, you'll have the ability to regulate the *Brush size, Strength and Smoothness, the Threshold, and Mask Advantage.* **Threshold** determines the effectiveness of the Mask, and Mask Advantage will help you to choose a razor-sharp or smooth advantage.

If you wish to pick a part of the foreground image that you need to make transparent, select, or pull your finger over the regions you want to mask. A red dot will be shown to enable you to understand and start to see the real place where you're focusing on:

- You'll additionally observe a pop-up. You can pinch out to focus on; to be able to get a far more in-depth view of small areas and fill up the region with an increase of accuracy. You can likewise pinch directly into zoom back to view the complete image.

- If you wish to view the areas you've masked more clearly, select the view masks icon (second icon at the very top right corner):

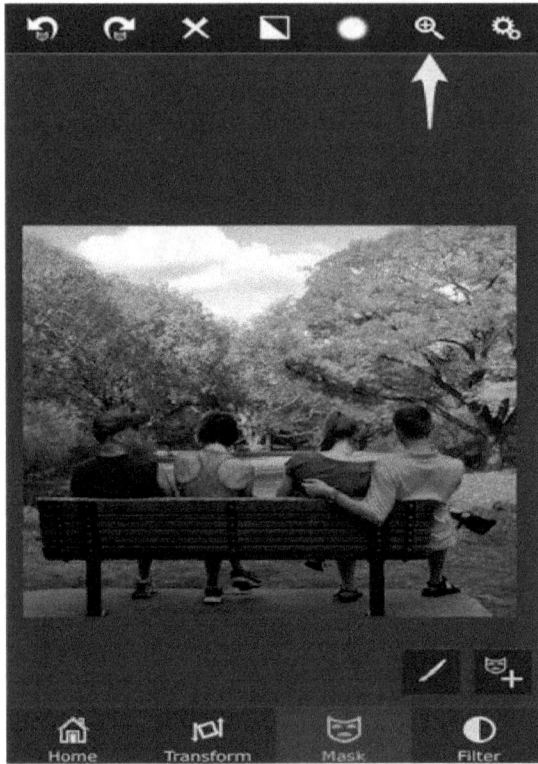

You will find four view masks alternatives that show exceptional colored backgrounds, as shown below (checkerboard, red, green, or blue color). This depends on the colors on your foreground picture because some colored backgrounds will screen your selection flawlessly.

You can maintain focus on masking your film at the same time by using the colored masks views, or you might change to regular pictures where you can view the background image as you Tap the View Masks icon near the top of the display.

Save Your Valuable Masks

- After you've used the mask tools to ensure regions of your foreground image are apparent and transparent, departing merely the area of the image that you want to superimpose on the background, it's a perfect concept to store your masks in the Masks library.

- This is recommended because it will help you to apply that mask on some other focus on another photo. Moreover, if you're likely to superimpose the area of the foreground picture onto every other historical photo, you'll only be asked to mask the foreground photo once.

- You might then import it onto any background picture every time you want to utilize it, which can save you from needing to mask the parts of this image every time.

- This **Mask Library** is obtainable in the home segment of the app, Tap the home option at the low area of the screen. You can select the Save Mask icon (the middle icon at the top of the screen) to save lots of the **Mask** and then Tap **Save.**

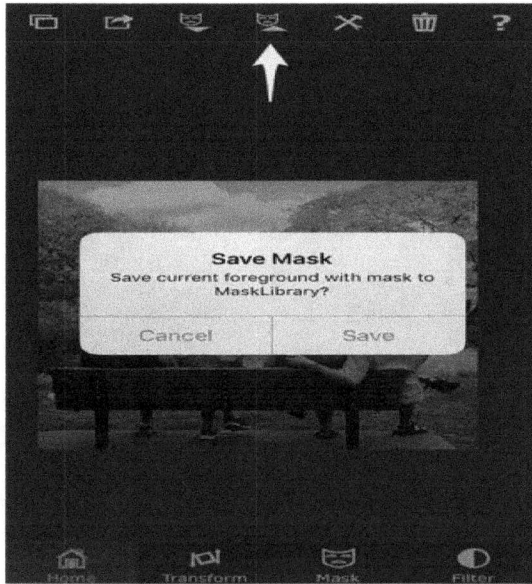

Whenever you're set to apply that masks again to a different background photo, Tap the **Load Mask** icon (third icon from the top left) in the **Home** section of the app:

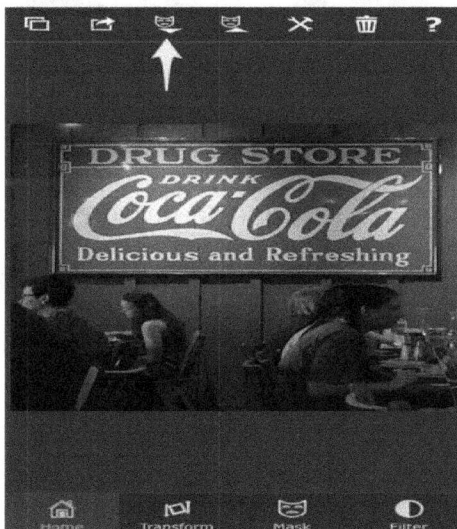

You'll now see the entire masks which you saved.

You can then Tap the masks you want to apply to place it onto your background image:

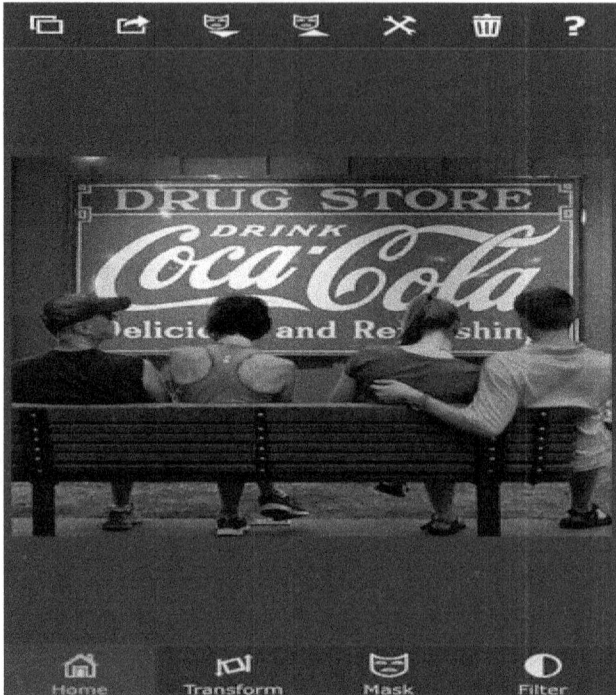

- **Save your Photo**

Whenever you're ready to save your final photograph, Tap the Export icon (second icon from the top left-hand side) in the Home section of the app. In the *Export Destination*, you can select photos to save the picture on your iPhone's photo library:

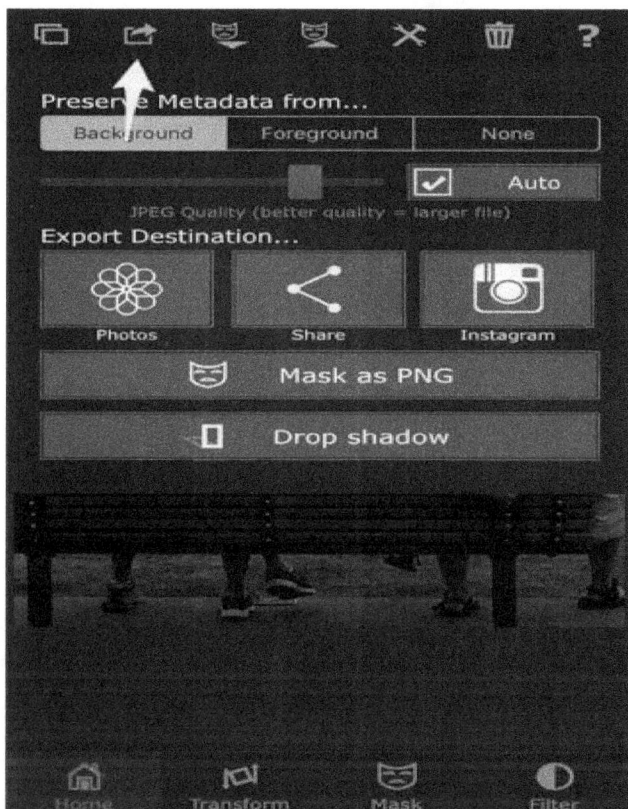

- **Delete the Session**

In case you choose to start the complete process again, Tap the Trash icon near the top of the display to delete the whole session to begin anew.

- **How to Produce a Double Exposure Picture**

Using the superimpose approach, you can also create an extraordinary increase in exposure impact. This calls that you should mix two pictures instead of masking one of these.

It's quite easy to develop great portraits with **double exposure silhouettes** just as the example below:

That is likewise an advantageous way for including a **texture overlay** to your image, which allows you to make a grunge look or textured painterly style. Below are the steps to check out to get this done;

Import Your Photographs

In the home portion of the superimpose app, use the import icon at the top right-hand side to import your background and foreground photographs precisely as you did with the first approach described above.

As both pictures are imported, the foreground picture can look similar to the background picture, as shown below:

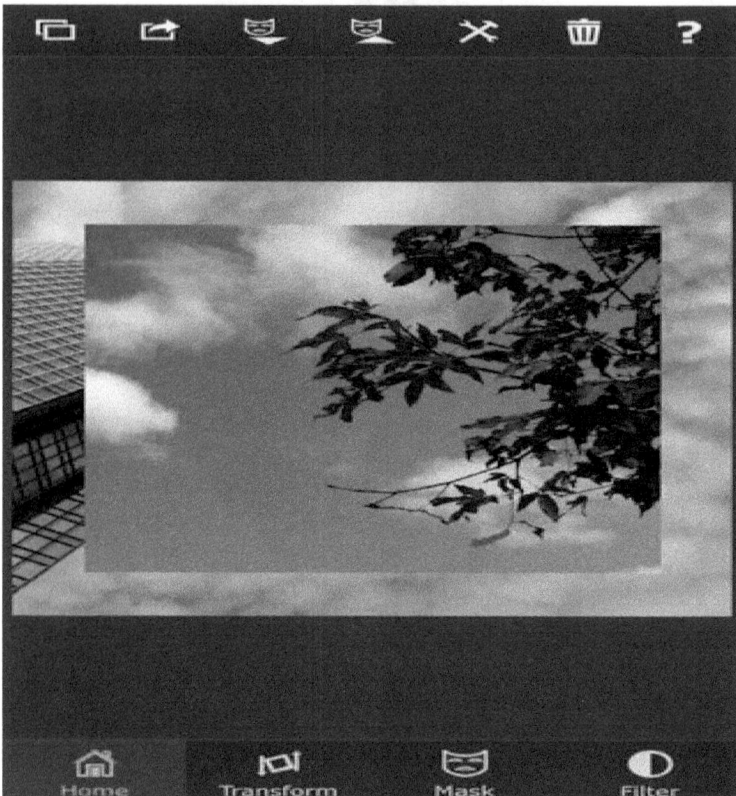

How to Blend the Pictures

You can start by Tapping the **Transform option** at the low area of the screen. This section is not limited by enabling you to reposition and resize your foreground picture; nonetheless, it additionally gives you access to change the transparency and mix mode.

To demand **Mix mode**, select the Settings icon at the very top right part of the display:

- **Mix mode** provides unique techniques; both pictures can also built-in together through the modification of presented tools such as comparison and brightness.

- The **Mix mode** is defined to default typically. It is one option to keep carefully the blend mode arranged to Normal and use the opacity slider to change the transparency of the foreground picture.

- Another approach is to see different blends of both pictures using a few of the other blend mode options, which consist of Multiply, Screen, Overlay, etc.

- You can merely Tap on the few different combination modes to observe how they have an impact on your final picture. Placing under consideration, the example below, Overlay, Colour, and Difference, was used. Each one of these creates a unique and fantastic mixture of both pictures:

How to Change the Filter

- Tapping the Filter option in the bottom of the screen will enable you to apply a growth of preset filtration system results to beautify the image. There are also adjustments presented tools for *color hue, saturation, exposure, brightness, comparison, color balance, and blur.*

- You might use these results to each one of the foreground and background images. It's a step that isn't usually necessary, but it's a false choice to have.

- Near the top of the display, choose whether you want to focus on the foreground or background image. Just select the configurations icon at the very top right part of the screen, and also you'll visit a pass on of adjustment configurations you can use:

Moreover, within the Filter segment, Tap the **FX** icon to access 33 distinctive preset filters, as shown below:

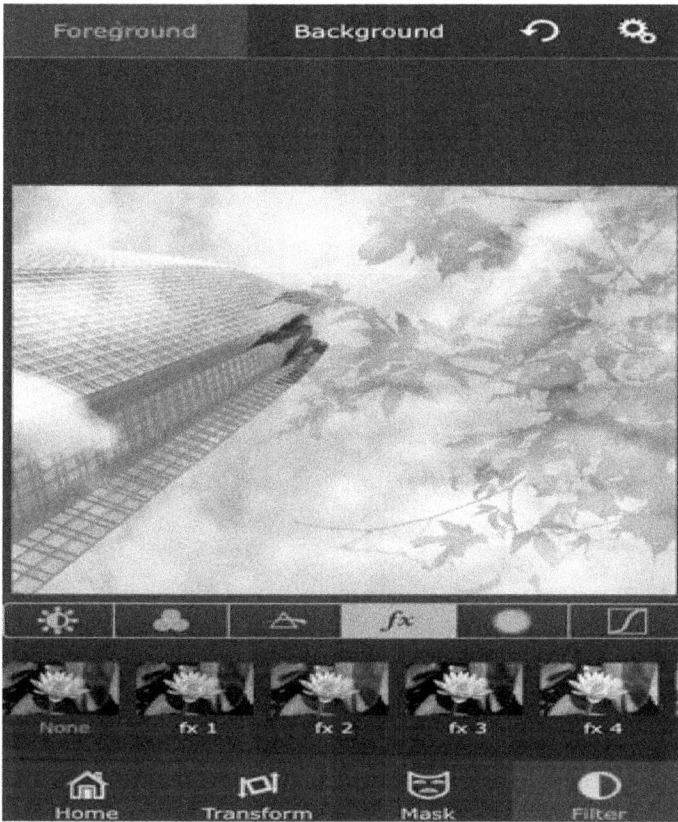

You can effortlessly change the filter on either of the pictures or both, creating unlimited blend feasibilities. Below are some examples of double exposure image with distinctive filters implemented:

When you've completed the editing process of your photograph, you can return to the home section to save your picture.

Summarily, superimpose is a remarkable app for changing backgrounds of pictures, in addition to creating outstanding double exposure photos.

- All you have is a foreground image and a background image, and next use the superimpose software to masks and mix both pictures as you wish.

- Whenever you've actualized the *perfect blend*, don't neglect to check the filters and adjustment modifications to see when you can further improve your picture with distinct effects.

Once you have mastered the utilization of the superimpose app, after that, you can try advanced layer masking techniques. You can likewise make sure you browse the Leonardo App, which is a product of the same company. Leonardo helps several layers, a big group of image modifications, in addition to other editing and enhancing tools.

Chapter 18

iPhone 8 Gestures You Should Know

Just like the iPhone 7 launched in 2017, the iPhone 8 doesn't include a physical home button, instead deciding on gestures to regulate the new user interface. It would require a couple of days to get used to the change but stay with it. By day three, you'll question how you ever coped without it, and using an "old" iPhone would appear old and antiquated.

1. **Unlock your iPhone 8:** Go through the phone and swipe up from underneath the screen. It truly is that easy, and also you don't need to hold back for the padlock icon at the very top to improve to the unlock visual before swiping up.

2. **Touch to wake:** Tap on your iPhone 8 screen when it's off to wake it up and find out what notifications you have. To unlock it with FaceID, you'll still have to set it up.

3. **Back to the Homescreen:** Whatever application

you are in, if you would like to return to the Home screen, swipe up from underneath of the screen. If you're within an application that is operating scenery, you'll need to keep in mind slipping up from underneath the screen (i.e., the medial side) rather than where the Home button used to be.

4. **Have a screenshot:** Press the power button and the volume up button together quickly, and it would snap a screenshot of whatever is on the screen.

5. **Addressing Control Centre:** It used to be always a swipe up, now it's a swipe down from the very best right of the screen. Even if your iPhone doesn't have 3D Touch, you can still long-press on the symbols to gain usage of further configurations within each icon.

6. **Accessing open up apps:** Previously, you raise tapped on the home button to uncover what apps you'd open. You now swipe up and then pause with your finger on the screen. After that, you can see the applications you have opened up in the

order you opened them.

7. **<u>Launch Siri</u>:** When you may use the "Hey Siri" hot term to awaken Apple's digital associate, there are still ways to release the function utilizing a button press. Press and contain the wake/rest button on the right aspect of the phone before Siri interface pops-up on screen.

8. **<u>Switch your phone off</u>:** Because long-pressing the wake/rest button launches Siri now, there's a fresh way for switching the phone off. To take action, you would need to press and contain the wake/rest button and the volume down button at the same time. Now glide to power off.

9. **<u>Release Apple Pay</u>:** Again, the wake/rest button is the main element here. Double touch it, and it would talk about your Apple Budget, then scan that person, and it'll request you to keep your phone near to the payment machine.

10. **<u>Gain access to widgets on the lock screen</u>:** Swipe from still left to directly on your lock screen, ideal

for checking your activity bands.

Using Memoji

- **<u>Create your Memoji</u>:** Open up Messages and begin a new meaning. Touch the tiny monkey icon above the keypad, and then strike the "+" button to generate your personality. You would customize face form, skin tone, curly hair color, eye, jewelry, plus much more.

- **<u>Use your Memoji/Animoji in a FaceTime call</u>:** Take up a FaceTime call, then press the tiny star icon underneath the corner. Now, tap the Memoji you want to use.

- **<u>Memoji your selfies</u>:** So, if you select your Memoji face, preferably to your real to life face, you can send selfies with the Memoji changing your head in Messages. Take up a new message and touch the camera icon, and then press that top button. Now choose the Animoji option by tapping that monkey's mind again. Choose your Memoji and tap the '*X*,' not the "done" button, and then take your picture.

- **<u>Record a Memoji video</u>:** Sadly, Memoji isn't available as a choice in the camera app, but that doesn't mean you can't record one. Much like the picture selfie, go to communications, touch on the camera icon and then slip to video and then tap on the superstar. Weight the Animoji or your Memoji, and off you decide to go.

iOS 13 iPhone 8 Notification Tips

- *Notifications collection to provide quietly*: If you're worried that you would be getting way too many notifications, you can place the way they deliver with an app by application basis. Swipe left when you've got a notification on the Lock screen and touch on Manage. Touch Deliver Quietly. Calm notifications come in Notification Centre, but do not show up on the Lock screen, play audio, present a banner or badge the application icon. You've just surely got to be sure you check every once in a while.

- *Switch off notifications from an app*: Same method as the "Deliver Quietly" feature, other than you tap the "Switch off..." option.

- *Open up Notification Centre on Lock screen*: From your lock screen, swipe up from the center of the screen, and you would visit a long set of earlier notifications if you have any.

- *Check Notifications anytime*: To check on your Notifications anytime, swipe down from the very best left part of the screen to reveal them.

Using Screen Time

- *Checking your Screen Time*: You can examine how you've been making use of your phone with the new Screen Time feature in iOS 13. You'll find the reviews in *Configurations > Screen Time*.

- *Scheduled Downtime:* If you want just a little help making use of your mobile phone less, you can restrict what applications you utilize when. Check out Settings > Screen Time and choose the Downtime option. Toggle the change to the "on" position and choose to routine a period when only specific applications and calls are allowed. It's ideal for preventing you or your children from using their cell phones after an arranged time, for example.

- *Set application limits*: App Limitations enable you to choose which group of applications you want to include a period limit to. Choose the category and then "add" before choosing a period limit and striking "plans."

- *Choose "always allowed" apps*: However, you might be willing to lock down your phone to avoid you utilizing it, that's no good if most of your way of getting in touch with people is via an application that gets locked away. Utilize this feature always to allow certain applications whatever limitations you apply.

- *Content & Personal privacy limitations*: This section is also within the primary Screen Time configurations menu and particularly useful if you are a mother or father with kids who use iOS devices. Utilizing it, you can restrict all types of content and options, including iTunes and in-app buys, location services, advertising, etc. It's worth looking at.

Siri shortcuts

- *Siri Shortcuts*: There are several little "help" the iPhone 8 offers via Siri Shortcuts. To start to see the ones recommended for you, go to *Configurations > Siri & Search* and choose what you think would be helpful from the automatically produced suggestions. Touch "all shortcuts" to see more. If you wish to install specific "shortcuts" for a variety of different applications that aren't recommended by the iPhone, you can do this by downloading the dedicated Siri Shortcuts.

iPhone 8 Control Centre Tips

- *Add new handles*: Just like the previous version of iOS, you can include and remove handles from Control Centre. Check out *Configurations* > *Control Centre* > *Customize Handles* and then choose which settings you would like to add.

- *Reorganize handles*: To improve the order of these settings, you've added, touch, and contain the three-bar menu on the right of whichever control you would like to move, then move it along the list to wherever you would like it to be.

- *Expand handles*: Some settings may become full screen, press harder on the control you want to expand, and it will fill the screen.

- *Activate screen recording*: Among the new options, you can include regulating Centre is Screen Recording. Be sure you add the control, then open up Control Centre and press the icon that appears like an excellent white circle in the thin white band. To any extent further, it'll record everything that occurs on your screen. Press the control again if you are done, and it will save a video to your Photos application automatically.

- *Adjust light/screen brightness*: You can activate your camera adobe flash, utilizing it as a torch by starting Control Centre and tapping on the torch icon. If you wish to adjust the lighting, power press the icon, then adapt the full-screen slider that shows up.

- *Quickly switch where a sound is played*: One cool feature is the capability to change where music is playing. While music is playing, through Apple Music, Spotify, or wherever, press on the music control or touch the tiny icon in the very best part of the music control; this introduces a pop-up screening available devices that you can play through; this may be linked earphones, a Bluetooth loudspeaker, Apple Television, your iPhone, or any AirPlay device.

- ***Set an instant timer***: Rather than going to the timer app, you can force press on the timer icon, then glide up or down on the full-screen to create a timer from about a minute to two hours long.

- ***How to gain access to HomeKit devices***: Open up Control Centre and then tap on the tiny icon that appears like a home.

iPhone 8 Photos and Camera Tips

- ***Enable/disable Smart HDR***: Among the new iPhone's camera advancements is HDR, which helps boost colors, light, and detail in hard light conditions. It's on by default, but if you would like to get it turned on or off, you manually can check out *Settings > Camera and discover the Smart HDR toggle change.*

- ***Take a standard photograph with HDR***: Right under the Smart HDR toggle is a "Keep Normal Photo" option, which would save a regular, no

HDR version of your picture as well as the Smart HDR photo.

- *Portrait Lights*: To take Portrait Setting shots with artificial lights, first go to capture in Family portrait mode. Portrait Setting only works for people on the iPhone 8 when capturing with the rear-facing camera. To choose your Portrait Setting capturing style, press and hang on the screen where it says "DAYLIGHT" and then move your finger to the right.

- *Edit Portrait Lights after taking pictures*: Open up any Family portrait shot in Photos and then tap "edit." After another or two, you will see the light effect icon at the bottom of the image, touch it, and swipe just as you did when shooting the picture.

- *Edit Portrait setting Depth*: Using the new iPhone 8, you can modify the blur impact after shooting the Portrait shot. Check out Photos and choose the picture you want to regulate, then select "edit." You will see a depth slider at the bottom of the screen. Swipe to boost the blur strength, swipe left to diminish it.

- *How exactly to Merge People in Photos app*: Photos in iOS can check out your photos and identify people and places. If you discover that the application has chosen the same person, but says they vary, you can combine the albums collectively. To get this done, go directly to the Photos application > Albums and choose People & Places. Touch on the term "Select" at the very top right of the screen and then select the images of individuals you want to merge, then tap "merge."

- *Remove people in Photos app*: Head to Photos App, Albums, and choose People & Places. To eliminate tap on "Choose" and then tap on individuals, you do not want to see before tapping on "Remove" underneath still left of your iPhone screen.

iPhone 8: Keyboard Tips

- *Go one-handed*: iOS 13's QuickType keypad enables you to type one-handed, which is fantastic on the larger devices like the iPhone 8 and XS Greatest extent. Press and contain the emoji or world icon and then keypad configurations. Select either the still left or right-sided keypad. It shrinks the keyboard and techniques it to 1 aspect of the screen. Get back to full size by tapping the tiny arrow.

- *Use your keyboard as a trackpad*: Previously, with 3D Touch shows, you utilize the keyboard area as a trackpad to go the cursor on the screen. You'll still can, but it works just a little in a different way here, rather than pressure pressing anywhere on the keypad, press, and hangs on the spacebar instead.

Face ID Tips

- *Adding another in-person ID*: if you regularly change appearance now, you can put in a second In person ID to state the iPhone 8 getting puzzled. That is also really useful if you would like to add your lover to allow them to use your mobile phone while you're traveling, for example.

iPhone 8: Screen Tips

- *Standard or Zoomed screen*: Since iPhone 6 Plus, you've had the opportunity to select from two quality options. You can transform the screen settings from Standard or Zoomed on the iPhone 8 too. To change between your two - if you have changed your mind after set up - go to *Configurations > Screen & Lighting > Screen Focus and choose Standard or Zoomed.*

- *Enable True Tone screen*: If you didn't get it done

at the step, you could transform it anytime. To get the iPhone's screen to automatically change its color balance and heat to complement the background light in the area, check out Control Centre and push press the screen lighting slider. Now touch the True Firmness button. You can even go to *Configurations > Screen and Lighting and toggle the "True Shade" switch.*

iPhone 8 Battery Tips

- **Check your average battery consumption**: In iOS 13, you can check out Settings > Battery, and you will see two graphs. One shows the electric battery level; the other shows your screen on and screen off activity. You would find two tabs. One shows your last day; the other turns up to fourteen days; this way, you can view how energetic your phone battery strength and breakdowns screening your average screen on and off times show under the graphs.

- **Enable Low-Power Mode**: The reduced Power

Mode (Settings > Electric battery) enables you to reduce power consumption. The feature disables or lessens background application refresh, auto-downloads, email fetch, and more (when allowed). You can turn it on at any point, or you are prompted to carefully turn it on at the 20 and 10 % notification markers. You can even put in control to regulate Centre and get access to it quickly by swiping up to gain access to Control Centre and tapping on the electric battery icon.

- *Find electric battery guzzling apps*: iOS specifically lets you know which apps are employing the most power. Head to Configurations > Electric battery and then scroll right down to the section that provides you with an in-depth look at all of your battery-guzzling apps.

- **Check your battery via the Electric battery widget**: Inside the widgets in Today's view, some cards enable you to start to see the battery life staying in your iPhone, Apple Watch, and linked headphones. Just swipe from left to directly on your Home screen to access your Today view and scroll until you start to see the "Batteries" widget.

- **_Charge wirelessly_**: To utilize the iPhone's wifi charging capabilities, buy a radio charger. Any Qi charger will continue to work, but to charge more effectively, you will need one optimized for Apple's 7.5W charging.

- **_Fast charge it_**: When you have a 29W, 61W, or 87W USB Type-C power adapter for a MacBook, you can plug in your iPhone utilizing a Type-C to Lightning wire watching it charge quickly. Up to 50 % in thirty minutes.

Chapter 19

15 Recommended iPhone Applications

<u>Spark</u>: Best Email App for iPhone 8

If you centre on iOS apps, you would understand that email has taken on something similar to the role of the antagonist in the wonderful world of iOS. App designers appear to know that everyone needs a better email platform, and they want an application to resolve their issues. Controlling email is just a little less stressful if you are using *Spark* as you would find features to suit your needs, such as; sending, snoozing email messages, and a good inbox that only notifies you of important email messages.

Below are the things you'd like about this application:

- The app is simple to use and socially friendly.

- Swipe-based interaction allows for one-handed operation.

What You may not like about it:

- No filter systems for automatically sorting email messages.

- The app does not have a way of controlling messages in batches.

Things: The best "To-do manager" for the iPhone 8

To-do manager applications are a packed field, and the application called *"Things"* isn't the only good one, and it is also not the only *to-do manager* on this list, but it's a carefully reliable tool, seated between control and hardy. The application provides the ideal levels of both control and hardy, without mind-boggling users to dials and without dropping essential features.

Things you'd like about this application:

- This app has a simplified interface that reduces stress when adding and completing the task.

- Tasks can be added from iOS with the sheet extension.

What you may not like are:

- Repeating tasks and deadlines can be buggy.

- Tasks can't be put into the calendar automatically.

OmniCentre: Best GTD-compatible To-Do App for iPhone 8

Like *"Things,"* **OmniCentre** is a favourite and well-designed to-do manager; however, they have a different group of priorities. Where **Things** attempts to remain simple and straightforward, **OmniCentre** is feature-rich and robust.

The application fully integrates with the **"Getting Things Done"** approach to task management called **GTD**, and this method stimulates users to jot down any duties they have, as well as almost all their associated information and scheduling. GTD users would finish up spending a great deal of time on leading end arranging work; because of this, the software takes a robust feature collection to implement all areas of the GTD process.

Things you'd like about this application:

- Most effective to-do list manager available.

- Can participate in virtually any task management style.

What you may not like:

- Sacrifices simpleness and usability for power and versatility.

Agenda: Best iPhone 8 App for Busy Notice Takers

Agenda requires a different spin on the notes application than almost every other application; its also known as *"date centred notice taking app."* Records are structured by task and day, and the times are a large part of the Agenda. Instead of merely collecting your jotting into a collection, Agenda creates a to-do list from *"things,"* with tight time integration, Agenda makes an operating journaling app and an able to-do manager and general iPhone 8 note-taking app. The day and note mixture seems apparent, but Agenda is the first iOS note-taking application to perform this mixture effectively.

It's a "to-do manager" and also a note-taking application with some calendar features, which enables seeing every information in a single place with one perspective and only one app. The application is also highly practical in the freeform, which may be uncommon in flagship apps. The beauty of the app *"Agenda"* comes out when using Pencil support, but for the present time, we'll have to turn to the iPad Pro for the feature.

Things you'd like about this application:

- Note-taking small tweaks can improve many workflows.

- The time-based organization fits most users; mental types of information organization.

What you may not like:

- Slow app release can limit how quickly you can write down a note.

1Password: Best iPhone 8 App for Security password Management

Using the auto-fill in iOS 13, *1Password* is as near to perfect as we have in a password manager. The Face ID authentication isn't unique to the iPhone 8 alone, but access Face ID makes the application better and simpler to use, which is an uncommon combination of accomplishments to reach concurrently.

Things you'd like about this application:

- Finding and copying usernames and passwords is extremely easy.

- Secure document storage space means *1Password* can gather all of your secure information in a single place.

- Auto-fill support finally makes security password management as easy as typing your security password.

What you may not like:

- No free version.

- The paid version uses membership pricing.

Twitterific: Best Tweets App For iPhone 8

Twitter is probably not the most exceptional sociable media system, but it's still one of the very most popular internet sites around, and like many internet sites, Twitter's default application is disappointingly bad.

Unfortunately, Twitter does lately nerf third-party Twitter clients. Third-party applications won't receive real-time stream notifications, significantly reducing the effectiveness of the applications; this move seems to pressure users to go to the native app, but considering its many defects, Twitterific and applications like it remain better.

Things you'd like about this application:

- Improves Twitter's visual demonstration dramatically.

- Includes smart and powerful features that make Twitter simpler to use.

What you may not like:

- Some organizational options are initially unintuitive.

- Twitter has purposefully knee-capped a good number of third-party apps, and Twitterific is no defence to those results.

Overcast: Best iPhone 8 App for Podcasts

Overcast is the best application you may use to hear podcasts. The app's user interface is considered carefully for maximal consumer performance, with features like "Smart Rate" which helps to intelligently manages a podcast's playback speed to shorten silences without accelerating speech, while Tone of voice Boost offers a pre-built EQ curve made to amplify voices, which is ideal for a loud hearing environment.

Things you'd like about this application:

- Thoughtfully designed interface for sorting and hearing podcasts.

- Features like Smart Speed and Queue playlists are invaluable once you're used to them.

- Active developer centred on avoiding an unhealthy user experience concerning monetization.

What you may not like;

- It most definitely doesn't seem to go nicely with the iOS lock screen.

Apollo: Best iPhone 8 App for Reddit

If you're thinking about *Reddit*, you would want to see the website beyond the third-party app. The application has improved, sure, but it's still kilometres behind third-party offerings.

Apollo is the best of the number as it pertains to Reddit clients, conquering out past champions like "Narwhal." Development is continuous and ongoing, with many improvements from the dev in the app's subreddit.

The swipe-based navigation would continue to work on any iPhone, of course, but it dovetails nicely with the iPhone application switching behaviour. The real black setting is also a delicacy for OLED screens.

Things you'd like about this application:

- Effortlessly handles an enormous variety of media.

- Well developed UI makes navigation easy.

- No ads in virtually any version of the app.

What you may not like:

- Sometimes is suffering from annoying and lingering bugs.

Focos: Best iPhone 8 App for Editing and enhancing Portrait Setting Photos

By default, the iPhone Family portrait Mode is a one-and-done process; you take the picture, and the blur is applied. iOS doesn't give a built-in way for editing and enhancing the Picture Setting effect following the fact. Focos fills the space, creating a tool to tweak both degrees of shadow and the blur face mask. It mimics the result you'd see when modifying a zoom lens' physical aperture. More magically, you can also change the centre point following the shot by recreating the blurred cover up on the different object, or by hand adjusting the result on the image's depth face mask instantly.

Things you'd like about this application:

- The most effective approach to manipulating Portrait Mode's depth-of-field effect.

- The depth map is a distinctive feature to help visualize blur.

What you may not like:

- Simple to make images look over-processed.

- Only about the centre, 50% of the blur range looks natural.

Halide: _Best iPhone 8 App for Natural Photos_

Distinctively, _Halide_ sticks essential info in the iPhone "ear." It embeds a live histogram for image evaluation; could it be precious? Nearly, but Halide is a near-perfect picture taking software besides that offering feature.

The settings are ideally positioned and configured, the RAW catch is pixel-perfect, and navigation within the application is easy and immediately understandable. If you are seriously interested in taking photos on your iPhone 8, _Halide_ is the best camera application for iOS.

Things you'd like about this application:

- Low handling power for iPhone photos.

- The broadest toolset of any iOS image editing and enhancing the app.

What you may not like:

- It can overwhelm first-time users using its degree of control.

Euclidean Lands: The Top-rated AR Puzzle Game for iPhone 8

Augmented reality applications haven't yet found their killer use. But AR gambling takes great benefit from lots of the iPhone features.

Euclidean Lands is a short fun puzzler that calls for the full benefit of AR's potential. Similar to Monument Valley, players manipulate the play space to produce new pathways through puzzle designs, guiding their avatar to the finish of the maze. The overall game begins easy; nevertheless, you might be scratching your head just a little by the end.

Things you'd like in this application:

- Challenging and attractive puzzle levels that take benefit of AR's unique features.

What you may not like:

- Disappointingly short.

- The core game auto technician feels very familiar.

Giphy World: Best AR Messaging App for iPhone 8

Plenty of applications have tried to usurp Snapchat as an AR messaging system. While Snapchat might maintain a weakened condition because of self-inflicted damage, it isn't eliminated yet. But if it can decrease, Giphy World is a great replacement.

Things you'd like about this application:

- Simple to create fun and funny images from provided assets.

- Content isn't locked inside the Giphy app.

What you may not like:

- Object place and processing speed are inferior compared to Snapchat's.

Jig Space: Best Usage of AR for Education on iPhone 8

Learning with holograms is one particular thing you

regularly see in sci-fi movies; with *Jig Space* and *augmented* actuality, that kind of thing is now possible in our daily lives. You should use the application to find out about various topics, including what sort of lock works, manipulating every part of the system, and looking at it from alternative perspectives. Jig Space requires the benefit of AR's three sizes effectively, and the low-poly models AR has bound not to harm the grade of the visualizations.

Things you'd like about this application:

- Takes benefit of AR's advantages for a good cause.

- A substantial assortment of "jigs" charges is free.

What you may not like:

- Accompanying captions are occasionally disappointingly shallow.

Nighttime Sky: Best Late-Night Outside Companion App

Directing out constellations is much more fun if you are

not making them up as you decide to go. *Evening Sky* was the main augmented-reality style application to seem on iOS. It shows just how for others on the system wanting to mimic its success, but it's remained dominant nevertheless.

Things you'd like about this application:

- It enhances the natural world with technology.

- It improves the star-gazing experience for both children and adults.

What you may not like:

- Large image units mean large camera motions are stiff and jerky.

Inkhunter: Most Readily Useful AR Gimmick on iOS

There's something distinctively exotic about checking out new tattoos by yourself. *Inkhunter* uses the energy of augmented truth to generate short-term digital symbols you can construct on the body and screenshot. You should use the built-in adobe flash, pull your designs, or import property from somewhere else to project on your skin.

Things you'd like about this application:

- Fun and book application idea that's useful.

What you may not like:

- Is suffering from AR's existing restrictions in surface matching.

INDEX

D

dark mode, **194**

Data, **50**

Depth of Field, *200, 227, 228, 229, 232*

digital cameras, **186, 191**

DO NOT Disturb, **29, 30**

DSLR, **226, 229, 234**

E

Email, **2**, **34, 35, 36, 37, 40, 319**

Eraser, 280

Euclidean Lands, 331

Exposure, **215, 217, 218, 254, 289**

F

Face ID, 32, 33, 34, 315, 324

Face Identification, **28**

FaceTime, *79, 80, 110*, **304**

Film, 236, 245, 248, 249

Filter, 295, 296

Filtering, **271**

fingerprint, **47, 48, 53, 59**

flash, **191, 236, 237, 240, 244, 245, 246, 247, 249, 250, 251, 252, 253, 258, 259, 266, 268, 310, 334**

Flash, 245, 248, 249, 251, 252, 258

Flash Auto, **258**

Flash On, **258**

Focos, **328, 329**

Focus, **215, 216, 217, 218, 228, 315**

Folders, **178, 181, 182, 183**

foreground, **200, 201, 216, 219, 228, 272, 274, 275, 276, 277, 278, 282,** **284, 285, 286, 291, 292, 294, 295, 296, 299**

frame, **186, 217**

FX, **296**

G

gestures, **301**

Giphy World, 332

GTD, 321

H

Hacks, *111*

HDR, **188, 218, 219, 220, 311**

HEIF, **187**

Hipstamatic, **236, 237, 238, 240, 242, 244, 250, 254, 256, 266, 268**

Hipstamatic Pro, 256

Home, **180, 182, 183, 271, 287, 288, 302, 317**

Home button, *156, 157, 163, 164, 165, 172, 180, 182, 209, 302*

I

iCloud, **32, 35, 37, 39, 40, 41, 42, 44, 49, 52, 53, 54, 56, 57, 58, 60**

iMessage, **43**

iMessages, *29, 43, 78*

Instagram, **186, 198, 199, 200, 201, 202, 203**

iOS 10, *140, 206, 210, 211*

iOS 12, *30, 77, 99, 104, 105, 107*

iOS 13, **30, 39, 193, 194, 195, 196, 305, 306, 314, 316, 324**

iPhone 11, **1, 28, 29, 30, 31, 34, 44, 56, 180, 185, 186, 189, 191, 218, 301,**